Vittorio Serra

ROME

2000 years of History and Masterpieces

The newly restored Sistine Chapel

New Edition

BET

BONECHI EDIZIONI "IL TURISMO" FIRENZE

Agent and distributor for Rome:
Gevi Service Italia S.r.l.
Via di Monteverde, 143
00151 ROME
Tel. and Fax +39-06.559.97.06

© Copyright 1999 by Bonechi Edizioni 'Il Turismo' s.r.l.
Via dei Rustici, 5 - 50122 Florence, Italy
Tel. (+39) 055.239.82.24
Fax. (+39) 055.21.63.66
E-mail: barbara@bonechi.com
        bbonechi@dada.it
http://www.bonechi.com
Printed in Italy

Managing Editor: Barbara Bonechi
Associate Editor and Picture Researcher: Lorena Lazzari
Proof reading: Dr. Giuliano Valdes, Editing Studio - Pisa
Layout and design: Lorenzo Cerrina
Cover and frontispiece: Nunzia Trabucco
Drawings on pages 6/7 and 18/19: Virgilio Galati
Photographic credits: Bonechi photo archives; Giuseppe Carfagna;
Nicola Quartullo; Marzio Marzot; Gennaro Pezzuti; Studio Novalux;
Antonio De Magistris; Arold Spindles; Photographic archives of the Vatican Museums.
Photo in the middle of the front cover: Nicola Quartullo
Photo-lithographs: Bluprint S.r.l., Florence
Printed by: Lito Terrazzi, Florence
ISBN 88-7204-415-4

* This guide book states where the various works of art were located at the time of printing.

A BRIEF HISTORY

*T*he famous legends relating to the foundation of Rome speak of Aeneas, Romulus and Remus and the seven kings. According to the myth, Romulus and Remus, sons of Rhea Silvia and the god Mars, were abandoned near the waters of the Tiber and nurtured by a she-wolf, la Lupa, who became the symbol of the city of Rome. In fact, in the Capitoline Museum in the Palazzo dei Conservatori the statue of la Lupa, an Etruscan bronze of the beginning of the 5th century B.C. is carefully preserved. Originally la Lupa stood alone; in fact, the charming figures of the twins were added by sculptor Antonio Pollaiolo in the 15th century. Scholars are not in agreement on the origin of the word Roma. Some claim that it derives from "Rumon" as the Tiber was called when the area was first settled, an event that took place on April 21st, 753 B.C. according to the Roman historian Varro; others believe the word to be a corruption of ruma (breast), the old name of the Palatine Hill which is, indeed shaped like a woman's breast. What we do know, however, is that sometime in the first millennium B.C. a Latin tribe settled the hill country around the Tiber Valley. The Latins were strongly influenced by the Etruscans whose 7th century B.C. domains extended over much of central and southern Italy, but by the 6th century B.C.. the Latins had prevailed over the Etruscans and became a sovereign nation with two great social classes: the plebes, and the aristocracy, or patricians, who ruled them. In the 5th - 4th centuries B.C. the plebes, led by their tribunes, managed to wrest power from their oppressors and civil and political equality was established. Once Rome had achieved a certain degree of political and social stability, it immediately became apparent that to keep her borders safe and her commercial supremacy intact she would have to extend her dominion over the surrounding territory and throughout Latium. The result was the creation of the Latin League and the swift defeat of her main rivals, the Sabines, the Equis and the Volscians. In the 4th century the city of Veii was conquered, but the Latins were in turn defeated by the Gauls who then sacked Rome. When they finally succeeded in regaining power in Latium, the Romans began a long campaign against the Samnites, the victorious outcome of which enabled them to create the most powerful domain in central Italy. The rise of Roman imperial power led to the inevitable decline of the Greek colonies in Italy and their gradual annexation as Rome extended her dominions from the Magra and Rubicon rivers south to the strait of Messina. Carthage, however, which dominated the Mediterranean and controlled strategic territories such as Sicily, Sardinia, and Corsica still stood in the way of Rome's great imperial ambitions and was far too close for comfort. At the end of the third Punic War, waged in 146 B.C. and won by the Roman general Scipio Emilianus, Rome defeated her great rival and the Carthaginian territory became a Roman province. Steady expansion of the Empire of course increased economic and industrial power and brought new riches to the Romans, but only to a minority of the population. This situation caused social unrest so serious that proletarian uprisings took place and finally the masses, led by Tiberius Sempronius Gracchus, a tribune of the people, rebelled against the patrician upper class. In 133 B.C. Gracchus was able to get a series of reforms passed, but they were never enacted due to the opposition of the rich landowners who had the tribune assassinated. His brother, Caius, however was elected tribune in 123 B.C., and, unlike Tiberius, was successful in getting important reforms enacted, e.g. Roman citizenship for all Latins, and the extension of Roman law to cover all the peoples living on the Italian peninsula. Around the middle of the 1st century B.C. Caius Julius Caesar, together with Crassus, proposed that the great landholdings be divided up, in order to alleviate the extreme poverty of the plebes and, at the same time, foster the growth of smaller individually-owned plots. The proposal, opposed by Cicero, was taken up by an ambitious politician, Lucius Sergius Catiline, who went even further, demanding that all past debts be cancelled and that the property of the rich be confiscated by the people – which, of course, greatly increased his popularity with the masses. Catiline however was defeated by the eloquence of Cicero, the people's militias he had organized were disbanded, and finally he himself was killed near Pistoia. After the long years of civil strife, a triumvirate composed of Caesar, Crassus and Pompey was set up and order was restored in Rome. Once he had been elected consul and had seen to it that the agrarian laws were finally enforced, Caesar took over the governorship of the three provinces of Gaul where the local inhabitants, Helvetians, Gauls, and Teutons, were planning an uprising against Rome, but they were no match for Caesar's military genius, and the rebellion was immediately put down. Meanwhile, back in Rome, Pompey, with the backing of the

Capitoline She-wolf (Capitoline Museums).

Senate, had become sole dictator after the death of Crassus. He ordered Caesar, who was on his way back from Gaul, to relinquish command of his legions. Not only did Caesar refuse to obey, he then proceeded to march on Rome at the head of the very legions he was supposed to have dismissed, forcing Pompey and his army to retreat to Greece. This event marked the end of Republican Rome and the beginning of the Roman Empire. Caesar accomplished what others before him had failed to do: he subjugated the Eastern provinces, restored peace in Asia and Greece, overcame Rome's last remaining enemies at Tarsus and in Spain, and also enacted major reforms affecting all facets of Roman life. But he also aroused discontent and jealousy, and, on March 15, 44 B.C., he was assassinated by Brutus and Cassius, whose purpose in ridding Rome of the tyrant had been, they said, to restore the Republic. Caesar's successors, Mark Anthony and Caius Julius Octavian, Caesar's nephew, defeated the troops of Brutus and Cassius at Philippi in Macedonia. But when Anthony marched to Persia to ward off the Parthians and then to Egypt where he formed an alliance with Cleopatra against the interests of Rome, Octavian had to employ not only arms but a series of astute political maneuvers just in order to maintain his power on the home front. . His first move was to try to gain control of the West, and when he succeeded, he set out to overthrow Anthony and Cleopatra in the East. When this, too, was accomplished (Anthony and Cleopatra, defeated in a sea battle at Actium, committed suicide) he returned to Rome where the Senate granted him the title Imperator, decreed him father of his country, and proclaimed him Augustus, i.e. the Divine, the name by which he is known to history. Under Augustus, from 8 B.C. to 9 A.D., peace and prosperity reigned throughout the Empire. During the period of Augustus' Pax Romana, Jesus of Nazareth was born in an outlying Roman province, Palestine, but this would not affect the Romans for a long time to come. Augustus was the first of the Imperial Age emperors and their dynasties, the Claudians, Flavians, and Antonines. Despite the fact that they all ruled as absolute monarchs, whose troops were called out whenever there was even a hint of an uprising or a revolt, the Roman emperors were not all tyrants. Surprisingly enough, a good number turned out to be valiant and oft times enlightened rulers.. This period, which lasted over two hundred years, from Tiberius (2nd century A.D.) to Constantine (4th century A.D.) was also the time when the "Good News" announced by Jesus Christ and preached by the Apostles Peter and Paul starting in the year 41, and thereafter by hosts of others, was slowly but steadily taking root and spreading throughout the Empire. Opposed until 313, when the Emperor Constantine and much of the Empire with him, was converted, Christianity would take over the political, judicial, cultural, and artistic heritage left by Roman civilization when the Empire ceased to exist in the 5th century. In fact, following the death of Theodosius the Great (the emperor under whose reign Christianity became the state religion), which occurred in 395 A.D., the Empire was split in two: the Roman Empire of the East which would last almost for another 1000 years, and the Roman Empire of the West, which ceased to exist after less than a century. The consequences of the division of the Empire were far-reaching in all fields. In the West the long series of barbarian victories began in 410 with the sack of Rome by the troops of Alaric. In 452 Attila started his march down the peninsula by razing the northern Italian city of Aquilea, but, upon reaching the banks of the Mincio River, he was somehow convinced by Pope Leo I to turn back. Even the help of the Roman Empire of the East was of no avail, and history records 476 as the date that Odoacer, King of the Vandals, became master of the whole peninsula. The influence acquired by the papacy during the barbarian invasions made it so that throughout the Middle Ages, the history of Rome is identified with that of the Catholic Church. By the 9th century, the power of the popes had grown so great that the Frankish king Charlemagne came to St. Peter's to be crowned Emperor by Leo III, an event which marks not only the birth of the Holy Roman Empire but the beginning of Rome's predominant role in European politics. In 1144 Rome became a city state; the ensuing power struggle between the Pope, the Municipal authority, the nobility, and the Emperor brought only political chaos and social unrest. In 1305, when the papacy was transferred to Avignon (1305 - 1377) there was a short-lived attempt to restore popular government in Rome, which was quickly stifled upon the return of the popes to Italy. From this time on, with the growing temporal power of the popes, Rome, in addition to being the center of Christendom, would also become a great cultural and artistic center. Papal policy was often not adequate for dealing with the difficult problems of the times; constant bickering, warring, power struggles, and religious schisms with the elections of popes and anti-popes took up a good deal of their time, nevertheless, some of the Medieval and Renaissance popes made outstanding contributions in

other fields: in 1420 Pope Martin V undertook the restoration of Rome, Eugene IV convened the Council of Florence in 1439 in an attempt to reunite the Latin Church with the Orthodox church, Nicholas V, who reigned from 1447 to 1455, was an erudite Humanist, who looked on helplessly as the Christian Empire of the East collapsed with the fall of Constantinople; Calixtus III promoted the Crusade against the Turks and the erudite Pius II Piccolomini of Siena famed for his great learning, was instrumental in founding the universities of Basil, Nantes, and Ingolstadt; Paul II enacted major reforms; Sixtus IV was an astute politician who was active in the defense of Christendom against the encroachment of the Moslems; his successor, Innocent VIII was a great patron of the arts; Alexander VI another great art patron, promoted the founding of missions for the spread of Christianity; Julius II della Rovere was a warrior pope, dedicated to the cause of Italian independence and a patron of the arts; the Medici pope who succeeded him, Leo X, was a great art patron and astute politician who failed, however, to arrest the advance of the Protestant Reformation. The second Medici pope, Clement VII, like his predecessors a promoter of the arts, looked on helplessly as Rome was sacked by German mercenaries in 1527. After this tragic event, Rome entered the period of the Counter-Reformation; during the papacy of Paul III (1534-1550) and Paul IV (1555-1559) the Council of Trent was convened and lasted for eighteen years; the Dominican saint, Pius V was pope during the battle of Lepanto; Gregory XIII, has gone down in history for the reform of the calendar; Sixtus V dedicated a good part of his papacy to the urban planning of Rome; and the Florentine, Urban VIII enacted reforms of the clergy, seminaries, prayer books, promoted missions and was a patron of the arts. Generally speaking, the 16th and 17th century popes tried to maintain a neutral stance in the power struggles being waged by European states. This changed when the effects of the French Revolution (1789) began to be felt in the Vatican, making the already shaky temporal power of the papacy appear about to topple. In 1797, Napoleon's troops invaded Italy. Rome was proclaimed a republic while the reigning pope, Pius VI, was carried off to France where he died on August 29, 1799. His successor, Pius VII, Barnaba Chiaramonti of Cesena was able to re-establish papal authority, due mainly to the change in Napoleon's political policy. With the decline of Napoleon's power a period ensued which was outwardly uneventful, but undercurrents of change were inexorably at work. In 1846, under Pius IX, the first uprising in favor of Italian unification received the enthusiastic support of the Romans who were firmly convinced that Pius was on their side, since his first official act as pope was to proclaim a political amnesty and freedom of press and speech. This impression was mistaken: Pius had no political aims, and was only interested in religious matters. Nevertheless, he accepted a patriot, Count Terziano Mamiani, as minister, but soon the political tide changed, and Mamiani was forced to resign. His successor, Pellegrino Rossi, a reactionary, was assassinated by revolutionaries, whose next act was to storm the Vatican and demand a constitution and the proclamation of a republic. The ambassadors of France and Bavaria helped the pope to flee to Gaeta on November 24, 1848, where he stayed as a guest of the King of Naples. The patriots lost no time and on February 9, 1849, the Constitution of the Republic of Rome was issued and the temporal power of the pope declared over. However, the newborn Republic, headed by a triumvirate (Giuseppe Mazzini, Aurelio Saffi, and Carlo Armellini), and defended by a company of Lombard soldiers commanded by Giuseppe Garibaldi himself, was short-lived. The French sent 8000 reinforcements who had no trouble overpowering Garibaldi's outnumbered troops, and the pope returned to Rome on April 12, 1850. But all was not lost for the independence movement. After 10 years of skillfully conducted diplomatic and military maneuvers, Count Camillo Benso di Cavour of Torino succeeded in having the Kingdom of Italy proclaimed on March 17, 1861. After Cavour's death, the Italian government, which in the meantime had transferred the capital from Turin to Florence, could act with complete freedom, since the pope's allies, the French, were at war with Prussia. General Raffaele Cadorna and 50,000 troops were ordered to take the Papal State. On September 19, 1870 they attacked, and a day later, through a breach in the walls at Porta Pia made by Cadorna's artillery, the Bersaglieri triumphantly entered the city, and Rome was proclaimed the capital of Italy with Victor Emanuel II of Savoy its king.. The pope, barricaded himself in the Vatican, declared himself a political prisoner and refused to accept the Guarentige offered by the Italian government to regulate relations between church and state. His uncomprimising attitude was shared by all of his successors up to Pius XI. who signed the Concordat of February 11, 1929, which put an end to the "Questione Romana" with an agreement which met with mutual satisfaction and was renewed on February 18, 1984. Now, at the dawn of the third millenium, Pope John Paul II has declared the Jubilee for the year 2000.

Bas-relief with figures of Roman dignitaries (Roman Forum).

• THE ROMAN FORUM •

Of all the monuments in Rome the Forum is perhaps that which has been most directly involved in the life of the city and its urban development, since it united in a single area all aspects of the social, religious, economic and political activity of its citizens. The Forum extended for approximately one third of a mile in the valley lying between the Palatine, Capitoline, and Esquiline hills. Originally marshland, the area was reclaimed by the construction of canals (one of these later became the Cloaca Maxima, Rome's famous sewage system) which drained the water into the Tiber. When residential zones still existed on the slopes of the hills, business dealings were already being carried out in the Forum. The origin of the name forum appears to derive from *fores* i.e. outlying inhabited areas. When these areas were joined together as a single city, the Forum became its ideal and geographic center-point. Gradually businesses were moved elsewhere, and monumental buildings started to grow up around the area which, at the same time, was developing along the Vicus Sacra. These included temples consecrated to the major deities and famous deified Romans, basilicas for public gatherings and court hearings, the Comitium where the citizens met to elect their magistrates, the Curia where Senate meetings were held, not to mention the arches, trophies, and dedicatory columns commemorating glorious events. Among the trophies, the most famous were undoubtedly the *rostra*. These were the prows of defeated enemy ships used to adorn the tribune, known as the Rostra, where speakers harangued the crowd. From the tribune, Cicero read his famous oration against Catiline, and Anthony enthralled the Roman populace with his emotional eulogy after the death of Julius Caesar. The importance of the Roman Forum began to decline as that of the Imperial Forums grew and then, during the Dark Ages, the Barbarians invaded the Roman Empire and the forums were looted and partially destroyed. In the 19th century with the birth of modern archeology, systematic excavations were conducted in the Forum area. Many interesting structures still survive in the Forum; on the following pages we will mention those which best exemplify its three fundamental aspects: the political, the administrative and juridical, and the religious. In any case it would be unfair to neglect the decorative structures like the Triumphal arches of Tiberius and Septimius Severus, the statues, dedicatory columns, tabernacles, shops, public conveniences, fountains and minor buildings.

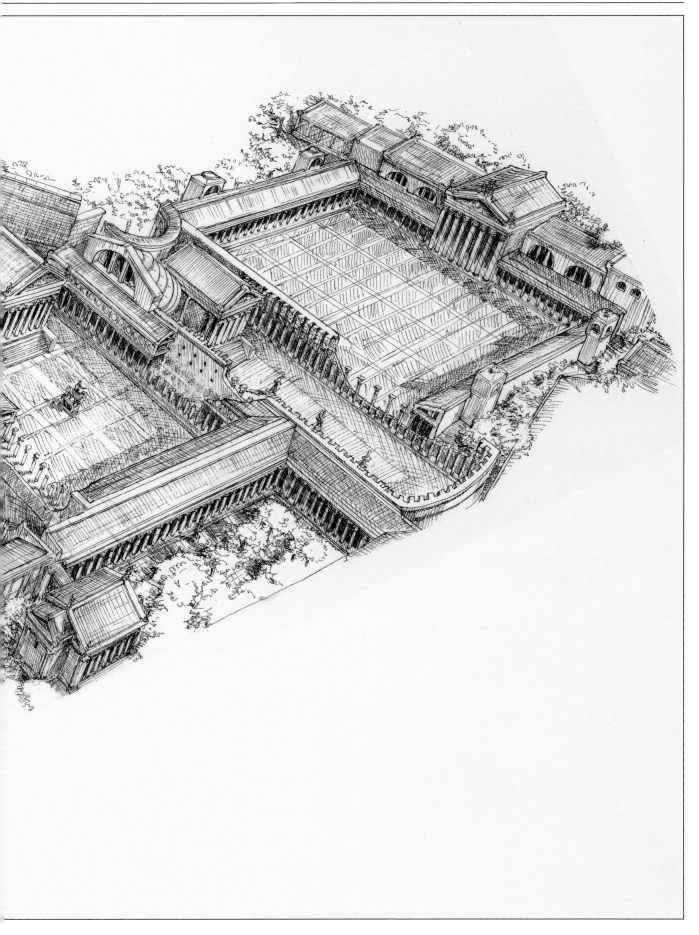

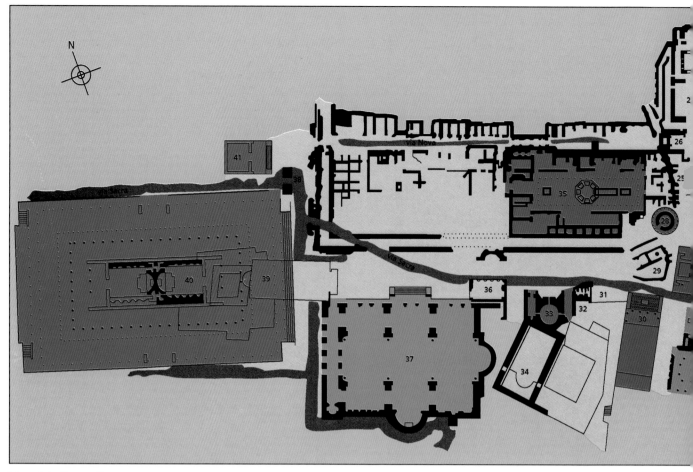

Map of the Roman Forum.

Arch of Septimius Severus.

•ARCH OF SEPTIMIUS SEVERUS•

The arch, built in 203 A.D. to commemorate Septimius Severus and his sons, Caracalla and Geta, is one of the largest in Rome (75 feet wide). The inscriptions on the sides of the attic recall Septimius Severus' victories over the Parthians, Arabians, and Adiabens. The bas-relief carvings above the smaller arches depict *Episodes from the Three Wars*, while *Barbarian Captives* are represented on the column plinths.

Detail of the bas-relief.

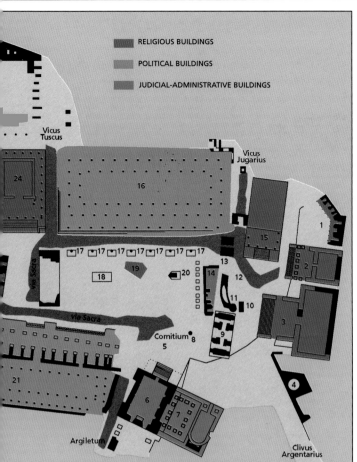

1	Portico of the Dii Consentes	24	Temple of the Dioscuri
2	Temple of Vespasian	25	Shrine and fountain of Juturna
3	Temple of Concordia	26	Oratory of the forty martyrs
4	Mamertine prison	27	Bibliotheca Pacis (Church of S. Maria Antiqua)
5	Comitum	28	Temple of Vesta
6	Curia	29	Regia
7	Secretarium Senati	30	Temple of Antoninus and Faustina
8	Lapis Niger (the Black Stone)	31	Pre-Roman burial grounds
9	Arch of Septimius Severus	32	Inn
10	Altar of Vulcan	33	Temple of Romulus
11	Umbilicus Urbis Romae	34	Church of Saints Cosmas and Damian
12	Miliarium Aureum	35	House of the Vestals
13	Arch of Tiberius	36	Medieval portico
14	Rostrum of the Caesars	37	Basilica of Maxentius and Constantine
15	Temple of Saturn	38	Arch of Titus
16	Julian basilica	39	Church of S. Francesca Romana
17	Honorary columns	40	Temple of Venus and Rome
18	Equestrian statue of Domitian	41	Temple of Jupiter Stator
19	Lacus Curtius		
20	Column of Phocas		
21	Basilica Aemilia		
22	Temple of Caesar		
23	Arch of Augustus		

• BASILICA AEMILIA •

All that remains of what was one of the largest Republican-period buildings are a few decorative elements, crumbling columns, capitals, and fragments of façades and lintels. It was built alongside the Curia in 179 B.C. by the Censors Marcus Aemilius Lepidus and Marcus Fulvius Nobilior, and then enlarged by other members of the Aemilia gens. The building was immense – the front with its portico facing out on the Forum extended 325 feet. The interior was divided into rooms, the largest being the hall (probably used for public gatherings), surrounded by a colonnade of African and gray-green Cipollino marble pillars.

• CURIA •

If tradition is to be believed, the Curia or Holy See was founded during the reign of Tullus Hostilius. It was destroyed several times by fire and was rebuilt in both the Republican and Imperial periods. It was used as a hall for the meetings of the Senate until the 7th century when Pope Honorius I transformed it into a church. Modern restoration has revealed its original plan, both inside and out, consisting of a simple rectangular hall with an inlaid marble floor.

Remains of the Basilica Aemilia.

• TEMPLE OF ANTONINUS AND FAUSTINA •

Commissioned by the Senate in 141 A.D. in honor of Faustina, wife of the Emperor Antoninus, who had been deified after her death. (It was later dedicated to her husband as well.) Only the beautifully decorated lintel construction resting on Corinthian columns remains of the original building, which was transformed into a Christian church in the 11th century and dedicated to St. Lawrence in Miranda; it was rebuilt in the 17th century.

• HOUSE OF THE VESTALS •

This was the residence of the six vestal priestesses, who were randomly selected by the *Pontifex Maximus* supreme religious head) from among twenty candidates aspiring to the sacred ministry. The Vestal virgins served for thirty years, during which time they were obliged to observe their vows of chastity and to make sure that the sacred fires never went out. Statues were dedicated to several priestesses of outstanding merit and piety and are still visible in the courtyard which originally had three pools in the center and was surrounded by a double colonnade.

The Curia; on the right, Statue of a Vestal Virgin.

Temple of Antoninus and Faustina.

Garden of the House of the Vestal Virgins.

•TEMPLE OF ROMULUS•

This temple was once believed to have been built by the Emperor Maxentius in honor of his son Romulus, who died in 307 A.D., but more probably Maxentius commissioned it as a reconstruction of the Temple of the Penates (household deities) which had been torn down to make way for the great Basilica. Most of the temple has survived since it was transformed into the atrium of the church of Saints Cosmas and Damian (6th century). The central chapel is still extant.. It was topped by a dome, had an arched façade, and was flanked by apse chapels on either side. The bronze door and its lock are both original.

•TEMPLE OF CASTOR AND POLLUX•

The temple, built in 484 B.C., was not only an important religious building but also a center of political activity: every July 15, the cavalry of the Roman army paraded before the censors outside the Temple, and, inside, newly-elected magistrates swore their allegiance and fidelity to the laws.

Today only the raised foundations (162' x 97') and three superb 39 foot-tall Corinthian columns, renowned for their majestic appearance and elegant form, are still standing.

Temple of Romulus.

Temple of Castor and Pollux.

• TEMPLE OF VESTA •

This was one the most sacred temples of ancient Rome, since the goddess Vesta was the protectress of the hearth and fire and as such symbol of the continuity of the State. Due to the fires which often broke out in the vicinity, it had to be restored and rebuilt several times. What we see today are the remains of the last restoration commissioned by Julia Domna, wife of Septimius Severus, in the 3rd century A.D. Its circular plan copied the shape of the old Italic huts made of wood and straw. The perforated cone-shaped roof served as a chimney.

• BASILICA OF MAXENTIUS •

Begun by Maxentius, the building was altered and completed by Constantine after he defeated Maxentius in the Battle of the Tiber at the Pons Milvius in 312 A.D. The original plan of Maxentius was for a single-aisled building whose nave was spanned by a single cross vault and whose aisles were covered by barrel vaults. The building was 253 feet long, 195 feet wide, and rose 114 feet at the nave. Constantine changed its original shape by opening a niche with an apse in the middle of the right nave and moving the main entrance.

Temple of Vesta.

Basilica of Maxentius.

• ARCH OF TITUS •

This arch, built to commemorate Titus' victory over the Hebrews, stands atop the Vicus Sacra at the forum exit. It was built after the Emperor's death, for, in fact, in the inscription Titus is called *divus*, a title the Romans reserved for their kings and emperors of special merit raised to the rank of demi-gods after death. Since Titus is known to have died in 71 A.D., it is generally dated late 1st century A.D. The single span structure is 50 feet tall, 44 feet wide, and 15 feet deep. The main structure stands on a tall base. It is adorned with Corinthian columns surmounted by a frieze depicting the triumphal procession of the victors. Winged Victories are sculpted on each of the four spaces above the pillars. On the inside are superb bas-relief carvings. One shows the Romans carrying off the spoils of war, among which the famous menorah (seven-branched candlestick) plundered from the Temple of Jerusalem, while opposite, Titus is represented driving a *quadriga* (chariot drawn by four horses).

• THE PALATINE •

The Palatine Hill, rising between the Roman Forum and the Circus Maximus, was most probably named after Pales, the goddess of the flocks, in whose honor the renowned Palilia festivities were celebrated. The Romans believed the Palatine to be the site of the city reputedly founded by Romulus on April 21, 753 B.C., and excavations conducted in the area have actually turned up the oldest settlements (9th - 7th century B.C.) discovered to date. During the Republican period, the Palatine became a luxurious residential zone which included the villas of Crassus and Cicero, and later, in the Imperial era, it was the site of some of Antiquity's most magnificent palaces and mansions.

The ancient road leading to the Palatine Hill; above, The Arch of Titus.

The great oval fountain (Palace of Domitian).

•STADIUM HIPPODROME•

The immense hippodrome or race-track on the Palatine (520' x 162') was built of brick and faced with marble. A portico ran round the exterior and on one of the long sides there was a special box from which the emperor watched the spectacles and races.

•PALACE OF THE FLAVIANS•

The *Domus Flavia* was built by Domitian in the late 1st century A.D. as his royal residence. It consisted of an immense basilica with three naves, the Aula Regia or throne room where the emperor held audiences; a *lararium* (shrine to the household gods) and a peristyle or colonnade, no longer extant.

Hippodrome of Domitian.

Circus Maximus as it appears today.

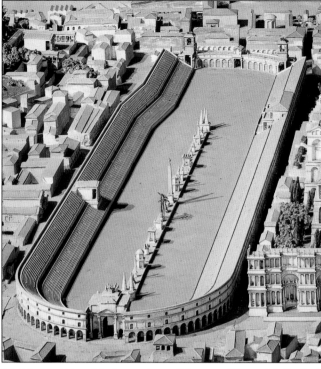
Model of the Circus Maximus as it was (Museum of Roman Civilization).

• DOMUS AUGUSTANA •

The Latin poet Martial described the Domus Augustana or house of the emperor as "one of the most beautiful things in the world". The original structure was built by Domitian (late 1st century A.D.). His successors, whose residence it was for centuries. enlarged and embellished it. In the Middle Ages. it was incorporated into other buildings and then in the 16th century, when the Villa Farnese and Orti Farnesiani (the residence and gardens of the Farnese family) were built, it was further transformed into a huge estate which still exists today.

• CIRCUS MAXIMUS •

According to legend, the Circus (an open oblong stadium used for chariot races) was built by the king of Rome, Tarquinius Priscus, where the famous rape of the Sabine women took place. Extending over an area approximately a third of a mile long in the valley once called the *Valle Murcia* between the Aventine and Pala-

tine hills, it was the largest of the Roman circuses, and served as a model for all those which followed. 200,000 spectators could thrill to chariot races, held fifty times a year in the Circus (up till 549, the year in which, under Totila, the last race was run). The low wall dividing the circus lengthwise, was called the *spine* and its two extremities *mete*. The spine was embellished with architectural elements of various kinds. One of them was the Egyptian obelisk now in Piazza del Popolo. The stands were originally made of wood, but after being destroyed several times they were rebuilt in stone. Julius Caesar's victory celebration of his African conquests, held in 46 B.C., was one of the most grandiose, ending with a mock battle fought by over 1000 foot soldiers, 600 mounted soldiers and 40 elephants.

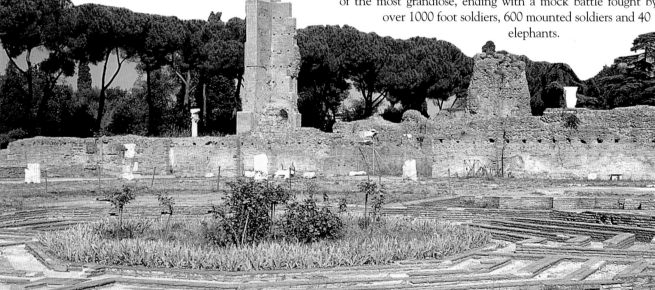
Octagonal maze fountain (Palace of Domitian).

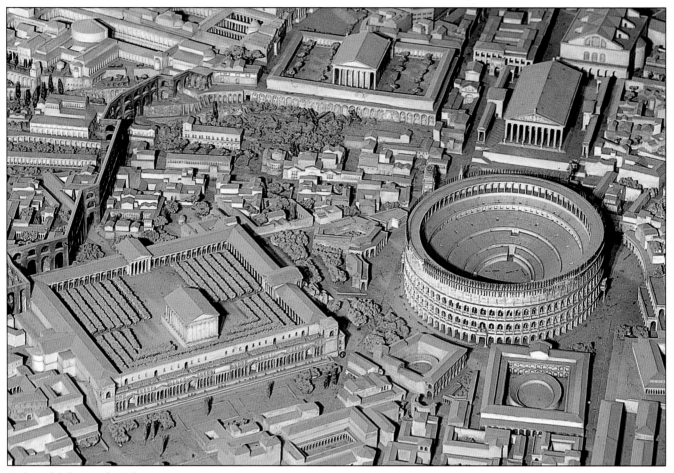

Scale model showing the Colosseum area as it was.

•COLOSSEUM•

The Flavian Amphitheater, better known as the Colosseum, rises majestically in the valley formed by the Esquiline, Celian, and Palatine hills. It was begun in 72 A.D. by Vespasian who filled in the man-made lake belonging to the golden house of Nero (*Domus Aurea*) to make way for it. The Romans were said to be pleased with Vespasian's project, because they had never really liked Nero's sumptuous palace which caused traffic jams and created an obstacle at the entrance to the forums. Also, in terms of esthetics and town-planning, the Colosseum was an ideal complement to the forum architecture, and served as a reference point for going to and from the other forum buildings. In 80 A.D., under Titus, the Colosseum was inaugurated with celebrations and spectacles, which, according to Martial, went on for 100 days and involved the deaths of innumerable gladiators and animals. Completed by Domitian and restored by Septimius Severus, the Colosseum has symbolized the grandeur of Rome throughout the centuries – in fact, in paintings, drawings and etchings, it is always depicted towering above the other Roman ruins. When Rome's thousandth anniversary was celebrated in 246 A.D. under the reign of the Emperor Decius, contemporary chroniclers tell of the slaying of 32 elephants, 30 lions, 40 wild horses, and dozens of other animals, including elks, zebras, tigers, giraffes, and hippopotami. There were also gladiator fights, the Romans' favorite spectacle, in which 2000 gladiators met their deaths. There is no historical proof, however, that Christians were collectively martyred in the Colosseum. Gladiator fights ceased in 404, although animal combats were allowed until well into the 6th century. Earthquakes damaged the building on several occasions. It was even turned into a fortress by two Roman families, the Frangipani and the Annibaldi. Only in 1312, by order of Harold VII of Luxembourg, did the Colosseum once more become property of the Roman people. In the centuries that followed it fell into decline as it was gradually dismembered and enormous blocks of travertine were hacked off it to be used for other buildings, among them Palazzo della Cancelleria, Palazzo Venezia, and even St. Peter's. In 1750, it was declared a shrine by Pope Benedict XIV since it was erroneously believed to be a site of Christian martyrdom.

EXTERIOR

The building is elliptical, 611 feet by 500 feet, and 185 feet tall. Construction went on for more than 10 years under the first three Flavian emperors: Vespasian, Titus, and Domitian. The name of its architect has not come down to us, but scholars generally attribute it to Rabirius, the celebrated

Model of the Colosseum (kept at the ampitheater).
View of the Colosseum.

Overview of the inside of the Colosseum.

architect of the Palace of Domitian. The four story outer structure was originally wholly of travertine. The first three levels consist of arcades composed of eighty round arches separated by semi-columns on pillars according to the classic sequence of Greek orders, i.e. the first level in Doric style, the second Ionic, and the third Corinthian. The fourth floor was a solid wall adorned with Corinthian pilaster strips and little windows. Holes are visible on the entablature running around the top of the structure; these were used for holding the staffs for anchoring the huge awning (*velarium*). Each arch of the ground-floor arcade was an entrance; 76 were numbered (the Roman numerals are still visible on the arches). The four main ones were reserved (and thus unnumbered), one for the court, one for Vestal priestesses, one for high-ranking officials and magistrates, and one for guests of honor. All the arches of the second and third floors were decorated with statues, although none of these have come down to us. When the Colosseum was used as a quarry for building material during the Middle Ages, all of the metal brackets anchoring the travertine blocks were removed, so that the building today appears full of holes. A colossal gilded bronze statue of Nero once stood in front of the amphitheater. The statue, almost 100-feet-tall, was known as the Colossus of Nero, and this might have had something to do with the name Colosseum.

View of the Colosseum.

INTERIOR

The Colosseum could hold from 50.000 to 70.000 spectators who were seated according to social class. There were three levels of seats: the *podium*, the lowest level, was for the upper classes and the emperor (who had his own box); the middle

Access arch from the cavea of the Colosseum.

Circular corridor under the cavea of the Colosseum.

one, for the *cives* or middle class people, while the highest from the ground, the *summa*, was for the masses. There was probably a fourth level for women Beneath the arena there were underground chambers, passageways, storerooms, dressing rooms, and maintenance centers which have now become visible because of the excavations.. This is where equipment and machinery were kept and where the animals were locked up before the shows. The main spectacles were the gladiator *ludi* (games) and *venationes* (animal hunts), but other kinds of performances were also put on, including jugglers' shows, athletic contests, jousts, and mock ship battles.

Games were held at regular intervals to mark both ordinary and extraordinary occasions. Ordinarily they were held on the Emperor's birthday and to mark historical dates; otherwise they were held to celebrate a triumph or a victory. Funerals were also occasions to hold a performance. Timely announcements (edicts), informed the public of the sort of spectacle, the reason for which it had been invoked and the day it would begin. The incredibly huge multi-colored linen and silk awning called *velarium*, was hoisted over the seating area by means of complicated equipment and employing hundreds of skilled laborers and provided a sunscreen for the spectators.

Corridors and steps in the Colosseum.

Arch of Constantine with the Colosseum in the background.

Temple of Venus and Rome.

•ARCH OF CONSTANTINE•

The Arch of Constantine was erected in 315 A.D. by the Senate and People of Rome (SPQR), as the inscription tells us, to celebrate Constantine's victory over Maxentius three years earlier. The triple arch structure is 60 feet high, 83 feet wide, and 24 feet deep, and is set off by four Corinthian columns. Many of its architectural and sculptural elements were taken from earlier monuments, such as the eight marble statues of *Barbarian Dacians* on the attic, which come from the Forum of Trajan, and the eight medallions with hunting and sacrificial scenes above the side arches, which date from the period of Hadrian. Not far from the arch once stood the *Meta Sudans* (traces of the base are extant). This was a cone-shaped fountain built in the 1st century A.D., whose few surviving remains were torn down in 1936. The existence of so many fountains and garden grottoes in Rome was made possible by the construction of the famous aqueducts like the *Aqua Giulia, Aqua Vergine, Aqua Claudia,* which may be considered masterpieces of Roman hydraulic engineering.

•TEMPLE OF VENUS AND ROMA•

The huge (357' x 172') building was erected between 121 and 136 A.D. by Hadrian in honor of Venus, mother of Aeneas. As Romulus and Remus were descended from Aeneas, Venus was worshipped as one of the mythical founders of the Roman lineage and thus of the city of Rome. The Emperor Hadrian himself drew up the plans. To make way for the building, it was necessary to move the Colossus of Nero which originally stood here (i.e. in the vestibule of the *Domus Aurea*). A double colonnade ran lengthwise around the building which stood on a raised platform. Midway along the colonnades were two small doors leading into the actual temple adorned with ten columns in front and twenty on either side. The result was a plan featuring two *cellae* each with its own apse, one dedicated to Venus facing the Colosseum and one to Roma in the Roman Forum. The temple was damaged by fire in 283 A.D., and was remodeled by Maxentius. The gilded bronze roof tiles were removed to be re-used in the old basilica of St. Peter's in the 7th century. All that is left today are the granite columns from the outer portico and the great apse facing the Colosseum.

Forum of Caesar.

•THE IMPERIAL FORUMS•

During the Imperial period, when the Roman Forum became too small to cope with all the public activities of an empire, it was decided during the era of Julius Caesar to build a new one. The Forum of Caesar was built from 54 to 46 B.C. and the other four forums followed. The new forums gradually supplanted the old Roman Forum, replacing it as the center of civic life and gradually appropriating all the activities which had taken place in the old forum, the Foro Romano.

•FORUM OF CAESAR•

The first forum in chronological order, this forum served as the prototype for all of its successors. It was rectangular in shape, with a portico on three sides having a double tier of columns, several of which are extant. Beneath the arcade were the *tabernae* (shops and businesses). One of the shorter sides was bounded by an

important building, the Temple of Venus Genetrix, which was commissioned by Julius Caesar in fulfillment of a vow he had made at the Battle of Pharsalus in 48 B.C. It celebrated Venus, mother of Aeneas and maternal ancestor of the Julian family to which Caesar belonged. The temple was adorned with masterpieces of Classical sculpture, including a statue of Venus by the Greek sculptor Archesylaos, two paintings by Timomachus of Byzantium, a statue of Cleopatra, pearls and gemstones.

Forum of Caesar;
to the left: *Statue of Augustus in the Via dei Fori Imperiali.*

Markets of Trajan; below: *detail of Trajan's Column.*

• MARKETS OF TRAJAN •

The Markets of Trajan were built to brace up the Quirinal Hill which looked as though it might collapse. The huge semi-circle had a protruding hall on either end, both of which are in excellent states of preservation. On the second level there are twenty-one shops. The third level is slightly set back with respect to the second and had an entrance from Via Biberatica, midway up the slope of the Quirinal, which also led to the main marketplace. On this spot was a huge rectangular two-story building spanned by six cross vaults resting upon pillars dividing it into twelve shops, six on either side.

This was most likely where bargaining and exchanges took place, and where foodstuffs were distributed to the poor.

The fish market, located on the top level, had both salt and fresh water tanks.

• FORUM OF TRAJAN •

The Forum of Trajan, designed by the celebrated architect Apollodorus of Damascus and erected between 107 and 113 A.D., is chronologically the last of the Imperial Forums. Only a tiny portion of what was the largest of the forums (975' x 600') is visible today (the rest is concealed beneath the asphalt of the Via dei Fori Imperiali). Entering by way of the Forum of Augustus, it was necessary to pass beneath the Arch of Trajan. Opposite the entrance stood the Basilica Ulpia which, with five naves, was the largest of the Roman basilicas (550' x 520'). It was also one of the most elaborately adorned and even its roof tiles were covered with gilded plates. On the other side of the forum were two libraries, one for Greek. and one for Latin, works. Not far from the libraries was a small courtyard in the middle of which rose Trajan's Column. Built in 113 A.D. to commemorate Trajan's victory over the Dacians, it was most likely designed by Apollodorus him-

Markets of Trajan.
On the right: *Trajan's Column.*

Columns of the Basilica Ulpia (Forum of Trajan).

self. All told, it is 124 feet tall, while its shaft measures exactly 100 Roman feet (97 of our feet), so that it was known as the Centenary Column. The sculpted scenes spiraling all the way up it (650 feet of them!) portray episodes from Trajan's war against the Dacians. 2500 figures are represented in the bas-reliefs which are considered among the great masterpieces of Roman art. The statue of St. Peter on top was raised in the 16th century to replace a statue of Trajan lost in the Middle Ages.

• FORUM OF NERVA •

The Forum of Nerva was built in 97 A.D. and was also called the *Foro Transitorio* because it was the main zone of transit connecting the forum area with the residential districts on the hill beyond it. The Temple of Minerva which stood in the middle was extant until the early 1600s when Pope Paul V tore it down so that he could use its marble for building the fountain of the *Aqua Paola* aqueduct. The remains of the two Corinthian columns near the temple site are known as the *Colonnacce*. They have been attributed to Rabirius, the architect of the Colosseum and the Palace of Domitian. The frieze bas-reliefs portray women's activities (which were protected by the goddess Minerva). Nearby are ruins of the so-called Noah's Ark. Remains of the Forum of Peace, built by Vespasian in 75 A.D. with the spoils of the Judaean War, are incorporated inside the Torre dei Conti and Church of Saints Cosmas e Damian, but most of the Forum is hidden under the asphalt of the surrounding roadway, the Via dei Fori Imperiali.

Forum of Augustus; below: lower portion of a column.

•FORUM OF AUGUSTUS•

Augustus, following the example set by his stepfather Julius Caesar, embarked on a huge renovation and building campaign, which naturally included a grandiose forum. Unfortunately, like Caesar's, very little of Augustus' forum is still in existence. The main entrance was through the Arch of the Pantanii. In the massive wall at the far end. One side of the 406' x 292' rectangle was made up of the Temple of Mars Ultor, erected in commemoration of the Battle of Philippi. A flight of stairs led from the forum up to the temple built on a tall base. On three sides ran an arcade of 49-foot-tall Corinthian columns of white Carrara marble, eight of which adorned the façade. A stairway led from the Forum plaza to the temple. Among the celebrated treasures originally displayed inside were two works by the famous Greek painter Apelles, an ivory statue of Apollo, Caesar's sword, and statues of Mars and Venus Genetrix. Originally, two marble covered basilicas containing a colossal statue of Augustus also stood in the forum.

•THEATER OF MARCELLUS•

This is the only theater of Roman antiquity that has come down to us. The theater had two levels of arcades with 41 arches on each level. What surmounted the first and second tiers (Ionic above Doric) is not certain; some say an attic, while others feel it was a Corinthian arcade – the same Doric-Ionic-Corinthian pattern that would later be masterfully used in the Colosseum. The theatre could hold up to 13,000 spectators. By 370 A.D., great blocks were already being removed from the stage and used for the restoration of a bridge, the Pons

Theater of Marcellus with three corner columns from the Temple of Apollo Sosianus in the background.

Cestius. The theater was then turned into a fortress by an aristocratic Roman family, the Fabi. Later, in the 16th century, the Savelli, another great Roman family, commissioned a famous architect, Baldassarre Peruzzi, to add another floor of apartments (finished, however, by the Orsini in 1712). Of the celebrated theater, all that remains is a section of the arcades and remains of some of the internal structures visible in the basement of Palazzo Orsini.

•TEMPLE OF VESTA•

The Temple of Vesta stood in what was once the Forum Boarium (present-day Piazza della Bocca della Verità, one of the most picturesque squares in the city). The temple is so named due to the fact that with its round shape it was similar to the temple dedicated to the goddess Vesta in the Roman Forum, but it was probably built in honor of Hercules Olivarius, the patron of the oil merchants' guild. The temple was erected under Augustus and is surrounded by a colonnade of twenty beautiful Corinthian columns.

Temple of Vesta (Forum Boarium).

•BATHS OF DIOCLETIAN•

Baths were an important part of Roman life. The Romans' free time was spent primarily in the stadiums and the baths. Not only did they swim in the huge pools and train in the gyms, they would also take strolls in the garden conversing with friends just to pass a pleasant hour or two after a hard day's work. The Baths of Diocletian were built between 298 and 306 A.D. and are extremely well preserved. They were the largest baths in Rome (measuring 1222' x 1173') and could hold up to 3000 people at one time. Around the main hall were reading rooms, libraries, gardens, and parks. The huge main *exedra* (now occupied by the Piazza della Repubblica) measured 468 feet in diameter. It served as a *cavea* (the semi circular seating area of ancient theatres), in which an audience could observe the athletes training. In 1563 Michelangelo built the church of Santa Maria degli Angeli over what had been the *tepidarium* (warm water bathing room). Today the Baths of Diocletian are occupied by the Epigraphy Section of one of the world's most outstanding museums of classical art, the Museo Nazionale Romano; since the early 1990s the main head-quarters of the Museum has been moved to the Palazzo occupied by the former Collegio Massimiliano Massimo.

Baths of Diocletian; below, *detail of a mosaic in the Baths of Caracalla.*

•BATHS OF CARACALLA•

The huge complex comprising the baths was begun by Septimius Severus, and inaugurated, still unfinished, by Severus' son, Caracalla, in 217. All but completed by Alexander Severus c. 230, it was later restored several times by various people including Theodoric. But the barbarian incursion led by Totila, devastated what had probably been the most immense monument in ancient Rome. Earthquakes, neglect, and abandon did the rest. The area covered by the complex totaled over 27 acres (1070' x 1060'). In front of the entrance on a street parallel to the Appian way, the former Via Nova (present-day Via delle Terme di Caracalla) there was a covered colonnade or portico housing shops and offices for the employees of the baths. The plan of the main building was the standard one used for all Roman baths: a central hall for the round *frigidarium* (cold baths), *tepidarium* (warm baths), and *calidarium* (hot baths) with other rooms such as gymnasiums, libraries. and auditoriums branching off it, and huge exedrae (semi-circular adjuncts similar to the apse of a church) on either of the short sides. The *calidarium* had a diameter of almost 114 feet and its dome rose a full 130 feet. Almost 2000 people could be accommodated at the same time. Many of the works of art once adorning it were discovered in the ruins and have found their way into museums. Among the best known are the so-called *Farnese Bull*, the statue of *Flora*, and the *Belvedere Torso* excavated in the 16th and 17th centuries. There were also superb mosaics, with both geometric and figurative designs depicting athletes, racing officials, and bathers, in an amazingly realistic style. Today, exhibitions and cultural events are held here in the summer season. From this description, brief as it is, we can surmise that the Roman baths were planned and built in compliance with the concept, still advocated by modern civilization, which is best summed up by the Latin motto: *Mens sana in corpore sano.*

Baths of Caracalla; below, right, *part of a column from the Area Sacra.*

Area Sacra of Largo Argentina.

•AREA SACRA DI LARGO ARGENTINA•

The Sacred Area is a small zone at the center of the Campo Marzio which is very important for its magnificent Republican era buildings. The Temple of the goddess Feronia is the oldest, dating from 217 B.C. It was peripteral, that is to say, surrounded by a single row of columns on a high podium. The columns were originally of tufa, a soft volcanic stone, which was later replaced with travertine. The Temple of Juturna was built shortly after that of Feronia, by Pompeo. During a subsequent restoration the columns in tufa also in this case were replaced with travertine. The Temple of the Permarine Lares is the largest. Erected in 179 B.C., it has also been restored in travertine. The Temple of Fortuna, the most recent and original, is circular in form and placed on a podium with columns in tufa and Corinthian capitals and bases in travertine. The vast flat area of the Campo Marzio once hosted numerous other buildings, among which theaters, public baths, etc.

Aurelian Walls near Porta San Sebastiano.

•AURELIAN WALLS•

The twelve miles of 12-foot-thick city wall were begun by Aurelian in 271 A.D. to defend Rome from the barbarian invaders, and finished by Aurelian Probus in 280. Every one hundred feet there was a square crenellated watch-tower, while round towers flanked the monumental entrance gates marking the beginning of the consular roads that connected Rome to the outlying cities of the empire. The walls were restored twice, first by Maxentius and then by Honorius, who reinforced the whole fortification. The most important gates were the Porta Maggiore (or Porta Prenestina), the Porta Appia (today known as Porta San Sebastiano), the Porta Pinciana, the Porta Flaminia, and the Porta Ostiense (or Porta San Paolo).

Remains of a tomb on the old Appian Way.

View of the old Appian Way.

•THE APPIAN WAY•

The famous roadway dates back to the beginning of Roman civilization. It was extended several times until reaching Brindisi (on the east coast) which was a major port for trade with the Orient. Originally, the road started from Porta Capena (hardly any of which is extant today). When the Aurelian Walls were built, its starting-point was moved to the Porta Appia later know as Porta San Sebastiano. The Appian Way is the best preserved of the consular roads – some of its paving even dates from Roman times. The first few miles are dotted with ruins of tombs, some of which still need to be identified. Proceeding along the Appian Way we note the ruins of the Mausoleum of Romulus, which the Emperor Maxentius built in honor of his son, Romulus, who died in 307 A.D. It consisted of a large open space enclosed within a great wall, around which ran an arched portico covered by cross vaults. Alongside the Mausoleum is the Circus of Maxentius which belonged to the huge Villa of Maxentius, ruins of which are visible on the north side. It is not much smaller than the Circus Maximus (1664' x 276'), and is much better preserved. There are also extensive remains of the semi-circular towers on the short side with the *carceres* which contained the twelve starting stalls for the chariots. The whole construction was slightly inclined so that the distance from the starting line would be the same for all the racers.

•TOMB OF CAECILIA METELLA•

This is the best-known and best-preserved of the monuments along the Appian Way. It was built in 50-40 B.C. for Caecilia Metella, daughter of the consul Q. Cecilius Metellus Creticus. In the 14th century, the tomb was turned into a crenellated tower and used as the keep of the Castle of the Caetani, which extends along both sides of the road; the medieval church whose remains are visible in front of the tomb was part of the castle. In the 17th century Urban VIII started to dismantle the tomb in order to remove building materials but he was forced to stop due to the protests of the Roman populace. The tomb is a cylindrical tumulus with a 65-foot diameter placed upon a high square base and was originally topped by a tall cone-shaped cusp torn down by the Caetani in 1302 when they added the brick crenellations. The frieze of festoons and bucranium (ox-skull motifs) on the top of the cylinder gave the area its name of *Capo di Bove* (Ox-head).

•THE CATACOMBS•

The term catacombs comes from the Latin *catacumbas* which means "near the descent to the tombs". Catacombs were used as burial places by the Christians from the first and the fourth centuries. Their entrances were always visible from the outside, until 250 A.D., year of the persecution

Tomb of Caecilia Metella.

A passage in the Catacombs.

Inscriptions and symbolic animals in the Crypt of St. Sebastian; below: Head of Christ (Catacombs of St. Calixtus).

by the Emperor Decius. The tombs encompassed long galleries which were sometimes as much as five stories high, as in the case of the Catacombs of St. Callixtus, the most impressive in Rome. The *loculi* or burial nooks which line the galleries are closed off by marble slabs, each bearing a simple inscription. There are 7, 5 miles of these galleries in the catacombs of St. Sebastian. It has been calculated that if the galleries of the fifty-two catacombs known in Rome were placed end to end they would cover a distance of 373 miles. All the catacombs are outside the walls in observance of the Roman law which strictly prohibited the interment or burning of corpses within the city. After the 5th century the Catacombs were no longer used for burials and became places of worship as attested to by the graffiti left by pilgrims on the tombs of martyrs. The catacombs are not only important for the information they give us about early Christianity, but also as fine examples of primitive Christian art.

•CATACOMBS OF ST. SEBASTIAN•

These catacombs are composed of four levels of tunnels. The crypt of St. Sebastian is located on the second level. Numerous early Christian inscriptions of allegorical animals are visible, each of which has a specific religious meaning.

•CATACOMBS OF ST. DOMITILLA•

These are the largest in Rome and their origins date back to the 1st century. They were built by St. Domitilla, niece of the emperor Domitian. The 4th century basilica built over the tombs of Saints Nereus and Achilleus and dedicated to them is of particular interest. It consisted of a large room originally with three naves and an apse, (only the columns remain, with beautiful sculpted capitals); the altar stood over the tombs of the martyrs and was decorated with a ciborium or canopy structure of which the small columns remain. The Flavian Hypogeum, a pagan cemetery from the 1st century B.C. belonging to the family of Domitilla, is well worth a visit.

Entrance to the Catacombs of St. Domitilla.

•CATACOMBS OF ST. CALIXTUS•

These catacombs consist of a series of innumerable and very complex mazes of tunnels – of which only 12,5 miles have been explored – to a maximum depth of 27 feet, on four levels. A 4th century stairway leads to the entrance to the catacombs. Immediately inside is the celebrated Papal Crypt with the tombs of the nine popes martyred in the 3rd century. Next door is the Crypt of St. Cecilia with 7th -8th century frescoes depicting St. Cecilia, St. Urban and a Head of Christ. There is a marble reproduction of the statue of St. Cecilia by Maderno over the tomb. Ahead lies a tall and spacious passage leading into the Cubicula of the Sacraments, containing symbolic 3rd century frescoes portraying Baptism, Penance, Holy Communion, etc. Other vast burial regions exist within the Catacombs of St. Calixtus which, along with sarcophagi and paintings of enormous interest, is thought to contain the tombs of popes Mark and Marcellinus and the hypogeum of Pope Damasus.

•THE CHURCHES•

*T*he advent of Christianity and its slow but steady spreading the Imperial era despite persecution and repression, was the cause of a radical change affecting both the mental outlook and social structure of ancient Rome. Constantine's official recognition of the new religion in the early 4th century B.C., marked the start of a new era. Christian basilicas began to spring up all over Rome, and it was natural that their style should reflect the influence of the pagan basilica, the Romans' public meeting places. Although the Barbarian invasions marked the end of Roman civilization, they failed to stifle the spread of the Christian religion. During the Middle Ages, while the grandiose buildings of pagan Rome were crumbling away, the churches of Christian Rome continually increased in both size and magnificence. The generous patronage and dreams of grandeur of the Renaissance and Baroque age popes led to even greater proliferation of new church buildings and much re-elaboration of existing ones, so that Rome's churches became and still are an integral part of the urban structure.

The Pantheon in an engraving by Pietro Datri (XIX century).

•PANTHEON•

This building, whose name means both "most holy" and "temple of all the gods", ranks as one of the great masterpieces of Roman architecture. The first version was a small rectangular temple built in 27 B.C. by Marcus Vipsanius Agrippa, son-in-law of Augustus. After it burned down in a fire in 120 A.D., the Emperor Hadrian decided to build another much bigger one on the same spot. Agrippa's name was left in the inscription, and the surviving columns were re-used as the new building's porch. A huge circular hall was added, and this architectural marvel has come down to us practically intact (except for slight breaches which appeared and were immediately repaired in the early 3rd century). During the Early Middle Ages, the Pantheon was left almost entirely untouched by the Barbarian invaders, and in the 7th century Pope Boniface IV turned it into a church, dedicating it to St. Mary of the Martyrs. The building is composed of the huge round hall preceded by a pronaos or inner portico which has eight columns in front and eight in back arranged so as to create

Piazza della Rotonda with the Pantheon.

three naves. The Corinthian columns stand over 40 feet tall and are made of Egyptian granite. Originally, the pediment and the portico both had decorations of gilded bronze, but in the 17th century Pope Urban VIII Barberini had them removed so that Bernini could use it for the baldaquin (canopy structure) he was erecting in St. Peter's (and thus the Roman saying, "where the Barbarians failed, the Barberini prevailed"). The interior is a perfect circle whose diameter and height are exactly the same (169 feet). On the lower level are seven full length niches, each of which has a pair of Corinthian columns and pilasters alternating with smaller rectangular niches surmounted by tympanums in the shape of an arch or a triangle. The second level consists of a row of blind windows alternating with squares. The hemispherical dome is the building's crowning touch. A remarkable optical effect is conveyed by the coffered ceiling with five rows of coffers each one slightly smaller than the one below it up to the great circular skylight or oculus (30 feet in diameter). Many famous Italians are buried here, among whom the first two kings of Italy (Vittorio Emanuele II and Umberto II), Queen Margherita, Raphael and the architect Baldassarre Peruzzi. This monument has been greatly admired by artists and scholars since Renaissance times. Michelangelo defined it as of "angelic and inhuman design".

Inside of the Pantheon.

Exterior of the apse of Santa Maria Maggiore; below: view of the basilica of Santa Maria Maggiore.

•SANTA MARIA MAGGIORE•
(Saint Mary Major)

According to legend, the Virgin appeared to Pope Liberius (352-366) one night in August telling him to build a church on the Esquiline Hill over a spot that he would find covered with snow the next day. When he awoke the Pope rushed to the Esquiline, where, to the amazement of all there was indeed a patch of snow, and ordered that a church be erected there. Thus, the church was also known in the past as Santa Maria della Neve (St. Mary of the Snow), to recall the legend concerning its founding. Actually, it was built in the mid-5th century by Sixtus III after the Council of Ephesus had officially ruled on the divine origin of the virgin birth of Christ. Despite continual modification and embellishment over the centuries, the overall effect of so many styles, one over the other or right beside the other, is actually quite pleasing to the eye, and in many cases creates effects of extraordinary beauty and originality. In front of the church, in Piazza Santa Maria Maggiore, stands a column which Pope Paul V had moved from its original site, the Basilica of Maxentius, in 1614. The majestic façade makes a striking backdrop to the square. The portico of the church has five openings surmounted by a loggia and behind the log-gia it is possible to see the mosaics of the original façade. The present day façade, designed by Ferdinando Fuga, was built in the mid-1700s during the papacy of Benedict XIV. One of the foremost Baroque architects in Rome, Fuga created an unusual effect by flanking the façade with twin structures. Inside the loggia, as mentioned, are the original 13th century mosaics narrating the legend of the Virgin of the Snow. The 14th century bell-tower is Rome's tallest (245 feet high). The interior of the church still gives the effect of stately simplicity typical of the Early Christian basilicas. Two rows of plain columns with Ionic capitals divide the central nave from the ones on the sides. According to tradition, the gilding on the superb inlayed coffered wooden ceiling (attributed to Giuliano da Sangallo) was fashioned with gold brought back from the first expeditions to the New World. The patterned marble floor dates from the 12th century. The conch of the apse is decorated with a large mosaic depicting the *Coronation of the Virgin with Saints*, executed by Jacopo Torriti in 1295. It represents one of the first examples of Gothic art in Rome. The façade of the apse, by Ponzio, dates from the time of Clement X (1676).

Basilica of San Giovanni in Laterano.

•SAN GIOVANNI IN LATERANO•
(Saint John in Lateran)

The oldest Christian church in existence, San Giovanni has always maintained its privileged status as the cathedral of Rome. The church was severely damaged by a terrorist attack on July 27, 1993. The name of the church derives from that of a patrician Roman family, the Plauti Laterni, whose sumptuous estate originally stood on the site. Recently, remains of huge Roman buildings have been excavated beneath the church. Nothing remains, however, of the original Early Christian basilica which, after being dedicated to the Saviour was later consecrated to St. John the Baptist and

View of the right transept with the organ (side entrance).

Cosmatesque Cloister of the Basilica.

View of the presbyterium of the Basilica.

St. John the Evangelist. The building we see today is the result of numerous remodelings effected over the centuries. For example one side bears traces of wall dating from the Early Middle Ages, whereas the bell-towers were built in the 13th century, and the secondary façade was erected by Domenico Fontana in 1586. The main façade was built in 1735 by Alessandro Galilei, a Florentine, after winning a competition called by Pope Clement XII. Its style marks the changeover from the Baroque to the neo-Classical style. The interior is also a mixture of styles and periods. The nave and aisles were designed by the great Baroque architect,

Francesco Borromini, for the Holy Year of 1650, but he left the 16th century transepts unaltered. At the crossing stands a superb 14th century tabernacle built by Giovanni di Stefano. In a separate building commissioned by Sixtus V for the Sancta Sanctorum, i.e., the pope's private chapel is the *Scala Santa* (Holy Stairs), erroneously believed to be the stairs from Pontius Pilate's palace which Christ climbed during the Passion week. Actually, they were originally part of the monumental staircase from the Lateran Palace, moved to the site for the purpose of providing access to the *Sancta Sanctorum* which contains important relics like the painting

The Scala Santa or Holy Stairway; below, right: Statue of St. Paul at the center of the quadriporticus of St. Paul's basilica.

of Christ which, according to tradition, was executed without human intervention and which has the power to ward off calamity. The cloister of the church was built during the years 1215-1232 by Pietro and Nicolo Vassalletto. two of the foremost marble craftsmen of the renowned Cosmati school which flourished in Rome from the 12th to the 14th century.

Overall view of St. Paul's Basilica.

SAN PAOLO • FUORI • LE MURA
(Saint Paul's Outside-the-walls)

Saint Paul's ranks after St. Peter's as the second largest church in Rome. Commissioned by Constantine in the 4th century, it was later enlarged by Valentinian II, Theodosius and Honorius. It is traditionally believed to rise on the site of St. Paul's tomb. Little, however, remains of the church's original basilica structure and decoration. Unfortunately, during the night of July 15, 1823, a fire broke out inside and the building was burnt to the ground. The few surviving remains were incorporated into the new

Basilica of St. Paul-outside-the-walls.

Remains of the original decorations in the cloister of the Basilica.

one built to replace it, which has little in common with the original, aside from its name. The imposing façade with its huge four-sided portico, today facing into Via del Mare, was erected at the end of the 19th century by Guglielmo Calderini. The statue in the center represents St. Paul. The tympanum over the façade is adorned with 19th century mosaics. Beneath the porch is a marble group of Saints Peter and Paul, by a 19th century sculptor, Gregorio Zappalà. The five-tier bell-tower built in place of the Romanesque original, has a rather odd shape. Saint Paul's, like the other patriarchal churches of Rome, contains a Porta Santa which is opened only during the Holy Years. The interior is vast but uninspired: although the eighty columns dividing the 429-foot-long structure into five naves are impressive for their huge size, they lack the stately beauty of those in the surviving Constantinian basilicas. Some of them, however, are original (from the Basilica Aemilia in the forum). The

The interior of the Basilica.

coat-of-arms of Pope Paul IX can be seen in the middle of the elaborate ceiling with its gold coffers on a white background. The mosaics in the frieze above the colonnade are portraits of all the popes starting with Peter. The majestic triumphal arch at the end of the nave is a fairly faithful replica of the original, and the mosaics are original (albeit restored). The arch was called the Arch of Galla Placidia as it was supposedly commissioned by the Byzantine empress. The mosaics, executed in the 5th century during the papacy of St. Leo Magnus, in the center represent *Christ in the act of blessing, with angels on the sides*, and on the sides are the twenty-four *Elders of the Apocalypse presenting crowns to the Savior*, with the figures of *Saints Peter and Paul* below. On the back of the arch there are still fragments of the mosaic decoration by Pietro

Cavallini from the ancient façade. These include *Christ with the symbols of the evangelists Luke and Mark and Saints Peter and Paul*. The main altar at the nave crossing is built over the tomb of St. Paul. The remarkable ciborium protecting it was executed by Arnolfo di Cambio in 1285. In the niches above the porphyry columns are *Statues of Saints Peter, Paul, Luke, and Benedict* with elegant bas-relief carvings. The impressive mosaic in the apse of *Christ blessing, surrounded by saints, apostles and angels*, was created by Venetian craftsmen around 1220. The cloister was finished in 1214, just before that of San Giovanni in Laterano which was also designed by Vassalletto. Particulary noteworthy are the composite columns above which runs a frieze of mosaic and marble inlay. Fragments of the original decoration of the basilica are displayed in the cloister.

Cloister of the Basilica of St. Paul's with coupled columns; above: apse area of the Basilica.

Detail of the tympanum with the Redeemer (San Paolo fuori le Mura).

Façade of the Church of San Pietro in Vincoli.

•SAN PIETRO IN VINCOLI•
(Saint Peter in Chains)

The church is also known as the Basilica Eudoxiana as it was commissioned by Eudoxia, the wife of Emperor Valentinian III, early in the 5th century. Still preserved inside the church are the chains used to restrain St. Peter in the Mamertine Prison in Rome, miraculously fused with the ones with which he was bound in Palestine. At the end of the 8th century, during the papacy of Hadrian I, the basilica was extensively restored, and modifications were also made during the Medieval and Renaissance periods. The five-arch porch was commissioned by Giuliano della Rovere and designed by Meo del Caprino around 1475. The upper section of the façade, whose only adornment consists of five windows, was built in the 16th century. The interior still maintains the stateliness of the great Early Christian basilicas. In the center of the 18th century coffered wooden ceiling by Francesco Fontana is a fresco depicting the *Miracle of the fusion of St. Peter's chains* by Giovan Battista Parodi. San Pietro is renowned for another reason – the great marble statue of *Moses* carved by Michelangelo in the right transept which was originally created for the Tomb of Julius II. It was supposed to have been much bigger, since it was intended for St. Peter's in the Vatican. Michelangelo spent three years working on it, from 1513 to 1516 but pope Leo X distracted him from the project giving him other commissions and the tomb as we see it was completed by pupils. The majestic figure of Moses enthroned in the lower part of the monument is, however, by Michelangelo himself and is ranked as one of the artist's greatest achievements. In this piece, Michelangelo's sculptural style has moved away from a strictly classical one and reflects the search for something more personal. The statue's grandeur underlines the power of the supernatural; the head, as well as giving a certain movement to the whole work, reveals a profound spiritual power in the penetrating eyes. (The same concepts of strength and energy are present in the Slaves, unfinished works, four of which are now in the Galleria dell'Accademia in Florence and two in the Louvre in Paris). In the Confessional in front of the main altar is a bronze urn containing *St. Peter's chains*. The tabernacle doors are adorned with beautifully-carved scenes from the life of St. Peter, by Caradosso. The sarcophagus in the crypt contains the mortal remains of the Maccabei brothers. Off the left aisle is the tomb of Cardinal Niccolò Cusano, one of the most learned Humanist scholars of the 15th century. In 1956, when the floor was being repaired, the remains of previous buildings were uncovered, some of which date back to the 2nd century B.C. These can be visited on request and entrance is gained from under the external portico. The School of Engineering of the University is to the right of the church, and inside there is a cloister attributed to Giuliano da Sangallo (1500) and a beautiful well, which was mentioned by Vasari.

Detail of Moses by Michelangelo; above, right: bronze urn with the chains of St. Peter.

Mausoleum of Pope Julius II.

Church of Santa Maria Aracoeli on the Capitoline Hill; below: interior of the church.

•SANTA MARIA D'ARACOELI•
(Saint Mary of the Heavenly Altar)

The church rises on the highest peak of the Capitoline Hill in the heart of Rome and, throughout the Middle Ages, it was considered the center-point of the city. It was built between the 4th and 7th centuries on the spot where the Tiburtine Sibyl supposedly predicted the coming of the Son of God to the Emperor Augustus. Her prophecy referred to a heavenly altar, the *Ara Coeli* of the church's name. The exterior was remodeled on several occasions, e.g. the present-day façade and the 122-step marble staircase leading up to it date from the 14th century, whereas much of the original interior is extant. The outstanding feature of the interior is the double colonnade comprising twenty-two Roman era pillars of varying sizes and styles dividing the church into three naves. The paintings, frescoes, and sculpture adorning it date from diverse periods, many from the Early Renaissance.

Church of Santa Maria in Cosmedin; below: the "Bocca della Verità".

• SANTA MARIA IN COSMEDIN •
(Saint Mary in Cosmedin)

This fine church was erected in the 6th century over a Roman building in a simple style and with simple materials. After being altered over the centuries, it was rid of its Renaissance and Baroque structures (including a fine 18th century façade) at the end of the 19th century by Giovan Battista Giovenale who was looking for the earliest structures; this restoration however resulted more in a remodeling than in a return to its original appearance. The interior is a mixture of arbitrarily reconstructed and rearranged elements from different periods and styles. The fine flooring, the 13th century ciborium, and bishop's throne in the apse were executed by Cosmati craftsmen. The sacristy contains superb frescoes of an Epiphany scene dating from the 8th century. Outside, beneath the portico, is the so-called *Bocca della Verità* ("mouth of truth"), a marble disk representing a face, which had probably served as a manhole cover. According to popular belief, anyone who tells a lie and then dares put his hand in the mouth will have it bitten off.

SANTA MARIA IN TRASTEVERE •
(Saint Mary in Trastevere)

Reputedly founded by Pope Julius I around the year 340, Santa Maria in Trastevere is one of the oldest churches in Rome and certainly the first to be dedicated to the Virgin. Like many others, it has been remodeled and restored over the centuries, although the greatest damage was done in the 19th century when mediocre murals were painted on the walls and figures believed to be pagan were removed from some of the capitals. In 1702, Carlo Fontana was commissioned by Pope Clement to add the impos-

Church of Santa Maria in Trastevere.

ing porch which covers the original 12th century façade containing a 13th century mosaic by Pietro Cavallini. The statues atop the railing are 16th century, while the bell-tower still retains much of its 11th century Romanesque appearance. Worthy of note in the interior are the mid-12th century mosaics decorating the apse by an anonymous artist; those narrating Episodes from the Life of Mary were executed by Pietro Cavallini.

• SANTA CECILIA IN TRASTEVERE •
(Saint Cecily in Trastevere)

According to tradition the church was built over the ruins of a Roman dwelling said to belong to Cecilia, a 2nd century Christian martyr. It was rebuilt by Pope Paschal I in the 9th century, altered many times after that, and restored on several occasions (most recently in 1955). The façade, like Santa

Church of Santa Cecilia in Trastevere.

Maria's, is a mixture of styles and periods. The portico is 18th century (designed by a Florentine, Ferdinando Fuga), the columns and architrave date from a 12th century remodeling, as does the Romanesque bell-tower, while the giant vase in the garden in front is an original Roman work. The interior has also been altered over the centuries, in some cases because restorations were necessary in others, because of changing styles and tastes. The central nave was remodeled in the 18th century, while in the 19th , the original colonnade had to be covered with reinforcing pilasters (still visible today), since it was feared that the building would collapse. Among the famous works of art in Santa Cecilia are the mosaic in the apse with Pope Pascal I, the ciborium carved by Arnolfo di Cambio in 1283, and the superb statue of St. Cecilia beneath the altar, sculpted by Stefano Maderno in the 17th century. Perhaps the most celebrated of all is the *Last Judgment* fresco in the adjoining monastery painted by Pietro Cavallini in 1293; it has unfortunately come down to us in poor condition.

• THE MUSEUMS OF ROME •

Rome has many fine museums containing a great quantity of priceless works of art; most of these started out as the private collections of great noble families such as the Colonna, Corsini, or Borghese and the Doria Pamphili. Others were created through lavish papal patronage, for example, the Vatican and Capitoline Museums. They contain an enormous amount of well documented art from Classical Antiquity. During the Middle Ages, Christianity imbued the entire artistic production with its concepts and

motifs, which later developed into the Byzantine, Romanesque and Gothic forms of art. The Renaissance and Baroque periods represent the high points in the artistic life of the city: a cultural center of international importance animated by papal patronage, Rome became the main reference point for the greatest artists in Europe from Michelangelo to Raphael, Caravaggio to Rubens and Bernini to Canova. The extraordinary artistic vitality of this era is apparent from the works displayed in the museums of Rome.

Judith and Holfernes by Caravaggio.

• THE GALLERIA NAZIONALE D'ARTE ANTICA •
(The National Gallery of Ancient Art)

Most of the works in the collection date from the sale of Palazzo Corsini to the Italian government in 1883. The Gallery, officially founded in 1895, was housed in Palazzo Corsini until 1949 when, due to lack of space (Palazzo Corsini also contains the National Academy of the Lincei) it was moved to Palazzo Barberini which had been acquired specifically for this purpose. The building is one of the finest Baroque palaces in Rome. The three foremost 17th century architects all had a hand in it; begun by Carlo Maderno and Borromini in 1625, it was finished some years later by Berni-

ni, who also designed its huge audience hall. The fresco of the *Glorification of the Barberini Family* painted by Pietro da Cortona on the ceiling of the Gran Salone, is the most famous of the many remarkable Baroque ceiling frescoes in Rome. 13th to 16th century works are conserved in Palazzo Barberini, while later works are still displayed in Palazzo Corsini. Of particular interest are: *Madonna and Child*, by Simone Martini. In contrast to Giotto's full-bodied solidity, Martini, a Sienese painter, proposes figures of refined delicacy, where the poetic message is entrusted to the skilful play of lines and the splen-

Saint Gregory the Great by Saraceni.

Saint Nicholas of Tolentino by Perugino.

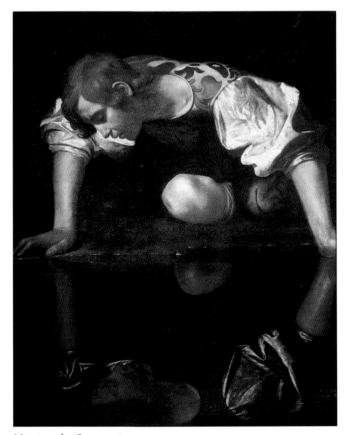

Narcissus by Caravaggio.

dor of the gold background. *Madonna and Child*, by Filippo Lippi (1406- 1469) . A Florentine artist of Masaccio's circle, he appropriated all his teacher's innovations and made them his own using a more intimate and sentimental language. *Madonna and Saints*, by Lorenzo Lotto. A Venetian painter of mixed artistic formation he brings together Venetian coloring and Roman and Durerian characteristics, as this picture clearly demonstrates. *Herodias*, by Guido Reni. Datable to around 1630, from late in this Bolognese painter's mature period. While the painting deals with a sacred and very tragic subject there is a predominance of nostalgia for the ancient, an adherence to classical ideals of beauty, and a search for stylistic refinement which characterized Reni's work during the last years of his life. *La Fornarina*, by Raphael. This famous painting has always been identified as a portrait of the woman Raphael loved. Executed around 1516, a few years before the artist's premature death, it is striking for its sweet idealization of womanly beauty, and fits into the pattern of the great painter from Urbino's lifelong attempt to represent classical ideals. *Venus and Adonis*, by Titian. Undisputed Master of an entire century of Venetian painting, Titian combined his own extraordinary ability with colors with the refinement of design characteristic of Mannerism in central Italy. *Christ and the Adulteress*, by Jacopo Tintoretto. Datable to around 1545, the canvas is part of the enormous production of sacred works by this Venetian artist. His preference for an "illuminist" use of color is also apparent

St. Mary Magdalene by Piero di Cosimo (Galleria Nazionale d'Arte Antica); below; *Satyr Resting (Musei Capitolini).*

Equestrian statue of Marcus Aurelius; below, from left: *Colossal statue of Hercules and an Amazon.*

here: the figures are almost sketches and nature is transformed; his refusal of the classical tradition is complete. Tintoretto, often misunderstood by his contemporaries, cleared the stage for Venetian Mannerism. *Ruins of the Baths*, by Giovanni Paolo Pannini. Born in Piacenza, Pannini arrived in Rome in 1711, and became famous as the author of wide perspective views of Roman ruins. *Portrait of Clement IX*, by Giovan Battista Gaulli, known as "il Baciccia" (1639-1709). A friend of Bernini, he became a favorite painter with the lay and ecclesiastic aristocracy in Rome. *Portrait of Stefano Colonna*, by Agnolo Bronzino (1503-72). Portraitist at the court of Cosimo I dei Medici, his subjects convey a static refinement.

• MUSEI CAPITOLINI •
(Capitoline Museums)

In 1471, Pope Sixtus IV donated a collection of antique sculpture to the city of Rome. His bequest was the start of the Musei Capitolini and represents the oldest public art col-

lection in existence. New works, mainly Etruscan and Roman sculpture, soon joined the original collection housed in the Palazzo dei Conservatori on the Campidoglio. In the 16th century several statues of Greek and Roman gods were transferred from the Vatican when Pius V decided to rid the papal collections of images of pagan deities, and, in the 17th century, a number of works were moved to the nearby Palazzo Nuovo.

In the 18th century, 300 years after its founding, the museum was officially christened Musei Capitolini. The collection continued to grow over the last two centuries, and had to be re-arranged, re-cataloged, and divided into sections.

Highlights in the museums include: *Bust of a Woman*, from the Flavian period (1st cent. A.D.). It was donated to the museums by Fra Giuseppe Fonseca former minister to King John V of Portugal. *Bust*, said to be of *Brutus*, from the 3rd -2nd century B.C. This unique example of Etruscan-Italic art, has enamel eyes which confer an expression of peculiar intensity. The *Capitoline Venus*, a 2nd century B.C. Hellenistic piece derived from a work by Praxiteles, it portrays the goddess leaving her bath. *Resting Satyr*, formerly at the Villa d'Este, was donated to the Capitoline Museums by Benedict XIV. It is one of the best replicas of the "Anapounemo" satyr by Praxiteles. *Amazon*, another donation of Benedict XIV. This ancient Roman copy is derived from the art of Phidias. Found headless, the new head has been remade imitating the features of a similar statue. The *Spinario*, or boy removing a thorn from his foot, from the Papal Palace in the Lateran. This piece is part of Praxiteles' work, which was so crucial in the development of Classicism in the Augustan era. *Bust of Commodus as Hercules*, rediscovered in 1874 in the Villa Palombara on the Esquiline. The Emperor Commodus (180-192 A.D.) is depicted with a lion skin, a club and the fruit of the garden of Hesperides in his left hand, in imitation of Hercules. Some other outstanding examples of Roman sculpture are: the 5th century B.C. bronze *Lupa capitolina* (the Capitoline She-wolf), perhaps the most famous symbol of the Eternal city, to which the two Twins by Pollaiolo were added in the 15th century and the marvelous statue of *Marcus Aurelius*. This famous equestrian monument was located in the Piazza di Campidoglio starting in the first half of the 15th century; it was subsequently moved to the Lateran, carefully restored in the 1980s, and afterward transferred to the Capitoline Museums in order to protect it from air pollution and weather.

Upstairs, the **Pinacoteca Capitolina**, the Capitoline picture gallery, contains

Sarcophagus with Greeks fighting Galatians.
Left: *Bust of a Roman lady.*
Center: *the Spinario.*
Below, left: *Bust of the Emperor Commodus as Hercules.*

the works of Italian and foreign artists of the 14th to 17th centuries, including: *The Holy Family*, by Pompeo Batoni. An elegant composition, with the bright and refined colors which characterized the works of the artist from Lucca (1774). *The Baptism of Christ*, a youthful work by Titian (1512), set in a poetic Giorgionesque landscape. The figure of Giovanni Ram who commissioned the painting can be seen on the lower right.

•GALLERIA BORGHESE•
(The Borghese Gallery)

The superb art collection assembled by Cardinal Scipione Borghese between 1605 and 1633 is still displayed in the Baroque halls of his palace. The collections of this museum are finally visible again after the restoration of the Casino Borghese was completed in 1998. During that time the picture gallery had been transferred to the buildings of the former Ospizio Apostolico of San Michele in Ripa Grande. Despite the fact that a number of works were carried off by the French during the Napoleonic period (and are still in the Louvre today), the collection has retained the characteristics of a private assemblage reflecting the tastes and preferences of its owner: in fact, there is a

The villa of the Borghese Gallery.

St. Jerome in his Study, by Caravaggio.

The Discovery of America, by Jacopo Zucchi.

preponderance of paintings by Bernini and Caravaggio, which demonstrates the great admiration Cardinal Borghese had for these two 17th century artists. The presence of others – Raphael, Dosso Dossi, the Venetians, Titian and Veronese, as well as a number of Flemish painters – is equally indicative. Of particular note are: *St. John the Baptist Preaching*, by Paolo Veronese. Part of Cardinal Borghese's collection since 1607, it is one of the artist's most significant works for its daring perspective which represents the episode at various levels and for the clear tonality of its coloring, often referred to as 'solar'. Gian Lorenzo Bernini was the undisputed Master of Roman Baroque. Sculptor, painter, writer and architect he placed his extraordinary talent at the disposition of the city's foremost noble families and the highest ranks of the ecclesiastic hierarchy. His fervid and creative imagination produced works of exceptional spiritual intensity and yet incorporated the more earthly and sensual aspects. This fundamental ambiguity permitted Bernini to paint both sacred and profane subjects. *The Rape of Proserpine* and *Apollo and Daphne* were part of a group of profane sculptures executed by Bernini between 1619 and 1625 for Cardinal Scipione Borghese. In both works the artist demonstrates his ability to incorporate features of Classicism into the free expression of his own creativity. *David* was executed for Cardinal Scipione Borghese in 1623. It took just

Paolina Borghese-Bonaparte, by Canova; below: David, by Bernini.

nine months. The biblical hero, a self-portrait of the young artist, is represented by a figure in movement, expressing Bernini's new concept of space in a vigorous and original manner. Here too is the celebrated *Pauline Borghese*, sculpted by Antonio Canova as Venus Victorious. Pauline was Napoleon Bonaparte's sister and the wife of the Roman prince who commissioned the sculpture in 1805, Camillo Borghese. It is one of the most significant works in Canovian Neoclassicism: Pauline, semi-nude, is depicted reclining on a magnificent Empire-style sofa, with the apple given her by Paris in her left hand to prove the superiority of her beauty. Canova's superb technique is apparent in the extreme care devoted to anatomical details, the hairstyle, the delicate decorations of the sofa and the smoothness of the marble. *The Deposition*, by Raphael purloined in 1608 for Cardinal Borghese from the church of San Francesco in Perugia. It dates from 1507, just before the beginning of the artist's Roman period, and bears witness to a moment in Raphael's career when he was obviously much influenced by Michelangelo. The *Sacra Conversazione*, by Lorenzo Lotto. Signed and dated (Laurent. Lotus MDVIII), the picture is closely connected with the polyptych of S. Domenico di Recanati. In its anti-classicism, Lotto's painting is related to certain

Northern schools and in particular to Durer who was in Venice during the first years of the 16th century. *The Archangel and Tobias*, by Giovanni Girolamo Savoldo. This work was purchased by the Italian state in 1911 and was not part of original Borghese collection. Contemporary critics agree on the picture's present attribution. The links with Venetian painting are evident, but the cold tonality and the metallic coloring of the characters and landscape point to a style peculiar to the painter from Brescia. *Sea Port*, by Paul Bril. Born in Antwerp (1554), Bril spent most of his life in Rome where he worked for various popes. He painted in the palaces and churches of Rome, executing frescoes of landscapes immersed in an atmosphere of poetic serenity. *Sacred and Profane Love*, by Titian, is considered one of the 16th century Venetian painter's youthful masterpieces. The picture's subject matter has never been definitely established, but it is thought to be inspired by the 'Hypnerotomachia Poliphili', a 15th century allegorical

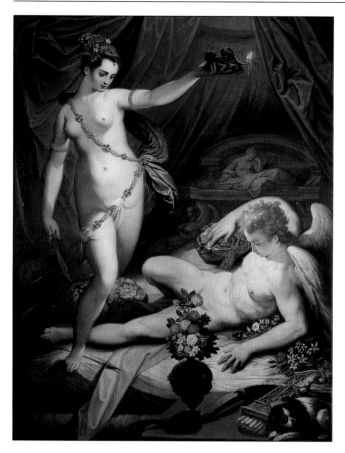

Boy with a basket of fruit, by Caravaggio (Galleria Borghese).
Left: *Eros and Psyche, by Jacopo Zucchi (Galleria Borghese).*

novel by Francesco Colonna. Michelangelo Merisi, known as Caravaggio after the name of his hometown, came to Rome around 1592. Contact with the cultured Roman environment and the patronage of rich noble families contributed to the enormous amount of work he was able to produce in his youth. At this time, the years of 'clear' painting, Caravaggio developed some of the characteristics which would come to typify his revolutionary stance in the face of artistic concepts of the period. He argued against the idealistic and the classical-style, which had degenerated by then into sterile, cold and monotonous repetitions of Raphael and Michelangelo's work. For Caravaggio painting was not empty rhetoric, heroic idealization of the past, or the artificial recreation of a poetic world: first and foremost, it was to be the most sincere representation of reality, indicate a rigorous moral commitment, and demonstrate an interest in piety expressed through humble figures. If we consider, for example, the *Boy with a basket of fruit*, typical of Caravaggio's youthful works, the light is still bright and diffused and illuminates an ordinary boy, certainly not rich, if we are to judge by his appearance. The intensity of the illumination is not used to give the boy a heroic stance, for the same dignity of pictorial subject is bestowed on the basket of fruit, situated in the foreground and expertly examined down to the slightest detail. Caravaggio was interested in precise representation, not as an empty exhibition of technical skill, but to guarantee an authentic link with reality. *Danaë*, a masterpiece by Correggio. Antonio Allegri, known as Correggio, developed artistically in an Emilian environ-

ment at the beginning of the 16th century, although his models were elsewhere, in Mantegna and Leonardo da Vinci. Perfection, both formal and in content were what his painting, and his classicism, aimed at. *Danaë* was part of a series of paintings with mythological subjects depicting *Jupiter's Lovers*, painted around 1530 for Federico Gonzaga, Duke of Mantova. *Portrait of a gentleman*, by Antonello da Messina. This is one of Antonello's most penetrating portraits, executed around 1474, when the artist was residing in Venice.

•THE MUSEO NAZIONALE ROMANO•
(The National Museum of Rome)

The museum was founded on February 7, 1889, in some of the rooms which were once part of the immense Baths of Diocletian and which had been formerly occupied by the Carthusian Convent of Santa Maria degli Angeli. The bulk of the collection comes from the bequest of a Jesuit priest, Kircher, works from the Antiquarium on the Palatine, pieces unearthed when the Tiber embankments were rebuilt, and, above all, Greek sculpture from the Ludovisi Collection (renowned for both the quantity and quality of its Greek originals). This latter collection is displayed separately in the Palazzo Altemps which is a remodeled 15th century structure re-opened for public use in 1997. Among the masterpieces of Roman sculpture are: the *Ludovisi throne*, the *Dying Galatian*, the *Orestes and Electra* group, and the *Ares Ludovisi* restored by none other than the

Entrance to the Museo Nazionale Romano; below: *detail of the Sarcophagus of Acilia.*

great Bernini. The main buildings of the National Museum of Rome are in the Piazza del Cinquecento (ex-College of M. Massimo) and the Baths of Diocletian now contain the epigraphy collection. The Museo Nazionale Romano is entirely dedicated to works of classical art and ranks as one of the best of its kind in the world. Outstanding works of art displayed here include: the *Tiber Apollo*, a Roman marble copy after a 5th century Greek original. The original work, for the classicism of its composition and extraordinary formal balance, has been compared to sculpture by the most important artists in the Greek world, from Phidias to Kalamis. It seems certain, however, that this piece comes from the last period of art in the 'severe style', characterized by the search for spiritual intensity in simplicity of form. The sculpture owes its name to the fact that it was rediscovered in the Tiber in 1891. The *Daughter of Niobe* from the Sallustian Gardens. This is a copy of a mid-5th century Greek original and is one of the first representations of the naked female figure in Greece. The original was part of a group of sculptures inspired by the tragic myth of the daughters of Niobe, killed by the arrows of Apollo and Artemis. The sculpture captures the dramatic moment when Niobe's daughter falls to the ground in a desperate effort to pull the divine arrow out of her back. The *Boxer*, a bronze Greek original from

the Hellenistic period. variously dated between 3rd and 2nd centuries B.C. It is attributed to Apollonius, Nestor's son, who also sculpted the *Belvedere Torso* preserved in the Vatican. Noteworthy, and typical of Hellenistic art, is the compelling realism of the representation: the boxer is depicted resting after a fight; his gesture, and stance are completely natural, every part of his body is rendered with anatomical precision and even the gloves are modeled with the same attention to detail. The fragmentary *Sacrophagus of*

Acilia, discovered at Acilia, between Rome and Ostia, in 1950, is datable to the first half of the 3rd century: the Severian age. The decoration consisted of a series of figures, placed at different levels: in the center, the deceased couple, to the sides, groups of muses and sages. The freedom of composition apparent in the placing of figures in relation to the space -ample and well-distributed - and the rendering of the hair, modeled with rapid strokes of the chisel, is characteristic of the sculpture of the Severian period. Some rooms in the museum have been dedicated to mural paintings, stuccos and mosaics with figures of animals, mythological scenes, etc. of immense interest.

Roman mosaic with animal figures; left, Niobe's daughter (Museo Nazionale Romano).

•GALLERIA DORIA PAMPHILJ•
(The Doria Pamphili Gallery)

This is one of the world's major private art collections and has remained practically intact over the centuries. Founded in the 17th century by Pope Innocent X Pamphilj, it was first enlarged by his descendants and thereafter by the Doria family when the Pamphilj line died out. The works, including paintings by Raphael, Carracci, Filippo Lippi, and Caravaggio, are still hanging in the positions chosen for them by their original owners in the huge family palazzo on Via del Corso. Worthy of particular note are: the *Bust of Innocent X*, by Bernini. One of the artist's last works, it reveals his extraordinary talent as a portraitist of refined technique, and

Rest on the Flight to Egypt, by Annibale Carracci.

Rest on the flight to Egypt by Caravaggio.

emphasizes his expert handling of light. *Herodias*, by Titian. This youthful work contains all the characteristics that later came to be typical of this artist: ample and harmonious forms, bright and luminous colors, and balanced composition amplified by the sky in the background.

Madonna and Child, by an artist of the Venetian School (Museo di Palazzo Venezia); below: Double portrait, by Giorgione (Museo di Palazzo Venezia).

MUSEO NAZIONALE
DI CASTEL SANT'ANGELO
(The Castel Sant'Angelo National Museum)

The museum was created in 1925, and occupies part of the historic building. Its astounding collection of arms and armor includes prehistoric arms, Greek and Roman helmets and shields, firearms of various periods, and even exotic weapons from the Orient. The equally fine art collection (painting, tapestries, sculpture, ceramics, furniture) is not to be overlooked. Some of the highlights are: *Bacchanalia*, by Dosso Dossi. This interesting work, which bears witness to his particular interpretation of the myth, won him the admiring praise of Vasari. *St. Jerome*, by Lorenzo Lotti. A sensitive and restless artist, Lotti was in contact with Venetian artistic circles, dominated by Giovanni Bellini. *Triptych*, by Taddeo Gaddi, a follower of Giotto for more than 24 years. This work, dated 1336, comes from the Museum of Naples. In its breadth of vision and brilliant coloring it reveals an affinity with Maso di Banco.

•MUSEO DI PALAZZO VENEZIA•
(Museum of Palazzo Venezia)

Since the end of World War II a collection of sculpture and decorative arts has been kept in the Museum of Palazzo Venezia. Small bronzes, porcelain, silver work, tapestries, precious enamels, ivories, etc. are displayed, together with paintings, and marble and wooden sculpture. Some of the most interesting pieces are: a 13th century

Madonna and Child. A wooden statue from Latium, in Byzantine style (Nikopeia or Hodegetria). This is a reliquary statue, i.e., a statue containing religious relics, most of which are contained in the big clasps sealing the borders of the Virgin's mantle. The polychrome brought to light by recent restoration is due to an ancient repainting (repeated with very little variation in color) over the original coloring, which has all but disappeared. 14th century *Processional Cross.* Executed in 1334, in gilded silver and decorated with enamels, it comes from the church of Santa Maria delle Grazie di Rosciolo (Abruzzo). *Finding of the infant Moses,* by Giuseppe Maria Crespi. The canvas (47" x 65") illustrates the biblical story in an 'archaic' manner common to a certain type of Venetian painting assimilated by Crespi during his visits to Venice. A delicate light makes the characters stand out over the brown tones of the background.

An Etruscan statue, the Apollo of Veio; left, the Madonna of Acuto, by an artist of the Latium School; below, from left to right: Phaliscan Bell-crater with scenes of the siege of Troy, and a bronze brazier with wheels.

•MUSEO ETRUSCO DI VILLA GIULIA•
(*Etruscan Museum of Villa Giulia*)

The museum was founded in 1889 as a collection of pre-Roman sculpture and artifacts from Latium (the province of Rome) and housed in Pope Julius III's 16th century villa. Shortly afterward, it was expanded to include the Etruscan works from the Barberini, Castellani, and other collections. In the 1950s it was completely renovated in keeping with the most advanced museum criteria. Of the many outstanding pieces, we shall indicate just a handful: the *Ficoroni Cista* (a superbly fashioned engraved bronze container for toilet articles), the *Veii Apollo* (a 6th century B.C. Etruscan sculpture), an Etruscan sarcophagus from Cerveteri, known as the *Sarcofago degli Sposi* dated second half of the 6th century, when the influence of Ionic art prevailed.

Nymphaeum of Villa Giulia (the Courtyard).

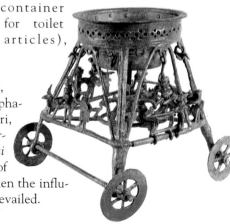

•MONUMENTAL ROME•

*T*he city's growth and development has always been greatly influenced by its past. The presence of monumental Classical ruins symbolizing Rome's past grandeur has been a constant reminder and stimulus to architects working in the city, encouraging them to aspire to similar heights. The destination of pilgrims from all over Europe, Rome had to live up to the splendid reports brought back by her admirers. As the center of the Christian world, the headquarters of the papacy, gradually sumptuous public and private buildings, fountains and gardens began to grow up everywhere in the city, whose beauty was further enhanced by countless tree-shaded avenues and charming piazzas. The 20th century has changed the face of Rome, capital of Italy since 1870. Modern buildings, mostly ministries and government agencies, and old palaces often stand side by side, not always in perfect harmony. Yet, although in many respects Rome has suffered the same fate as other contemporary European capitals, unlike them, it has never lost touch with its more than two thousand year history and with its 'vocation for the universal'.

Church of Santa Maria d'Aracoeli and the Campidoglio with its double stairway.

•THE CAMPIDOGLIO•

The heart of ancient Rome, the Capitoline Hill was the site of temples dedicated to Jupiter Capitolinus and Juno Moneta, two of the most popular of the numerous Roman gods. The square, redesigned as we see it today by Michelangelo in the 16th century, is reached by way of an imposing staircase, also by Michelangelo, from Piazza d'Aracoeli. The two Egyptian lions at the base are copies of the originals found in the Campus Martius and now in the Capitoline Museum, while the statues of Castor and Pollux and their horses, dating from the Imperial period, have been here since 1583 when they were excavated near the Theater of Pompey. One of the most striking features of Michelangelo's elegant design of the square is the decorative pattern of the paving stones. In the center is a copy of the bronze equestrian statue of the Emperor Marcus Aurelius haranguing the crowd. The original of this

Statue of the twins, Castor and Pollux at the top of the staircase.

Piazza del Campidoglio and Palazzo Senatorio.

statue stood here until 1981 when it was removed, restored and transferred to the Capitoline Museums. It stood in Piazza San Giovanni in Laterano before being moved here in 1583. One of the very few antique bronzes to have come down to us, it escaped being melted down and re-used in the Middle Ages because it was believed to represent the Emperor Constantine. Its influence on Renaissance art was considerable: 15th century masterpieces such as Paolo Uccello's John Hawkwood fresco in the Cathedral of Florence, Donatello's statue of Gattamelata in Padua, and Verrocchio's statue of Bartolomeo Colleoni in Venice all took the great statue as their prototype. The façade of **Palazzo Senatorio** makes an impressive backdrop for the square. Designed by Michelangelo, it was built by Giacomo della Porta and Girolamo Rainaldi between 1582 and 1605 in a rather altered form with respect to the original plan. The ground floor niche contains a statue of Minerva between personifications of the Tiber and the Nile. The 16th century bell tower was built by Martino Longhi the Elder. Above the clock are the bells that once summoned the populace to public assemblies. The building is entered by way of Michelangelo's double staircase. Inside are archeological finds relating to the Campidoglio and historic relics such as flags, coats-of-arm, banners, etc. Busts of famous historic personages (e.g. Raphael, Metastasio, Pius VII, Cimarosa, Canova, to mention a few) are displayed in the Sala della Protomoteca. They were carved by different sculptors in different periods. Twin buildings, the **Palazzo dei Conservatori** and the **Palazzo Nuovo**, flank Palazzo Senatorio. Like Palazzo Senatorio, they were designed by Michelangelo, but built by della Porta and Rainaldi. Both are important art museums. The collections include classical sculpture, decorative elements, and other archeological finds relating to

The Dioscuri and the stairway to the Campidoglio.

Equestrian Statue of Marcus Aurelius (copy).

ancient Rome. The museums, collectively known as the Musei Capitolini, are divided into six sections: the Capitoline Museum, the Museo dei Conservatori, the Sale dei Conservatori, the Braccio Nuovo. the Museo Nuovo, and the Pinacoteca (Picture Gallery).

• IL VITTORIANO •
(Monument to king Victor Emanuel II)

This enormous monument to king Victor Emmanuel II was built entirely in white limestone by Giuseppe Sacconi between 1885 and 1911 to celebrate Italian Unity. Though it is inspired by the architecture of Classical Antiquity it is an unfortunate example of an unsuccessful attempt to insert a modern structure in a classical context, the area of the Imperial Forums. A great staircase leads up to the *Altar of the Homeland* which contains, in a case in the center, the *Statue of Rome* between the bas-relief carvings of the *Triumphant Processions of Work and Patriotism*. Beneath the *Statue of Rome* is the *Tomb of the Unknown Soldier* built in 1921. Two additional staircases lead to the base of the equestrian statue of Victor Emanuel II in bronze (originally gilded) by Chiaradia and Gallori. On top is the immense portico which is surmounted by two bronze chariots with statues of the Winged Victory by Carlo Fontana and Paolo Bartolini (1908).

The Vittoriano, symbol of Italian unity.

Palazzo Venezia in the plaza of the same name.

Overall view of the Piazza del Popolo.

•PALAZZO VENEZIA•

Looking like some kind of medieval castle rising in the downtown section of the city, Palazzo Venezia is actually the first example of Renaissance architecture in Rome. The name of the architect who designed it in 1455 has not come down to us, although it is sometimes attributed to the great Florentine master, Leon Battista Alberti, known to have been working for Pope Nicholas V in Rome at the time. We do, however, know the name of the person who commissioned the building: Cardinal Pietro Balbo (later Pope Paul II). In the 16th century, it was used as the Embassy of the Republic of Venice. In the 19th century, it was taken over by the Austrians, and was not restored to the Italian government until 1916. Since the end of World War I, it has been a museum (Museum of Palazzo Venezia).

•PIAZZA DEL POPOLO•
(The People's Plaza)

The huge space between the Porta del Popolo (the old Flaminia Gate) and the intersection of Via del Corso, Via Ripetta, and Via del Babuino was designed in the early 1800s by Giuseppe Valadier, who combined old and new structures to create an unusual and dramatic setting. On the south side are the twin churches of Santa Maria di Montesanto and Santa Maria dei Miracoli, designed by Carlo Rainaldi.

Piazza del Popolo.

Palazzo del Quirinale; right: *the "Pulcino della Minerva".*

•PIAZZA DEL QUIRINALE•

The setting of the square is splendid. It rises on the top of the Quirinal Hill, the site of the Roman Temple of Quirinus. The statues of Castor and Pollux at the base of the Egyptian obelisk in the center come from the Baths of Constantine. On one side of the square is **Palazzo della Consulta**, the seat of Italy's Supreme Court. It was built by Ferdinando Fuga in 1734 as a court-house for the *Tribunale della Consulta.* The majestic Palazzo del Quirinale is the work of several architects, including Mascherino, Fontana, Carlo Maderno, and Bernini. Begun in 1574, it wasn't completed until around 1735. When Italy became a united kingdom at the end of the 19th century, it was used as the royal palace. It is now the official residence of the *Presidente della Repubblica.*

•PULCINO DELLA MINERVA•

The charming little marble elephant, forming the base of the 6th century B.C. Egyptian obelisk in Piazza della Minerva behind the Pantheon, is affectionately called *"pulcino della Minerva"* (the Minerva chick) by the Romans. Designed by Bernini for Pope Alessandro VII, it was carved by Ercole Ferrata in 1667. The church **of Santa Maria sopra Minerva** stands on the east side of the piazza. It was begun in 1280 in Gothic form by the Dominican friars, Sisto and Ristoro. The Renaissance façade is by Meo del Caprino (1453). The inside, with a three nave structure, contains numerous tombs of famous people and valuable works of art. To the left of the

main altar, the famous statue of *Christ bearing the cross,* by Michelangelo. Behind the altar, the tombs of Clement VII and Leo X, Medici popes, executed by the Florentine sculptor Baccio Bandinelli. In the left aisle, the tombstone of the painter Fra Beato Angelico (d. 1455).

•PALAZZO• BRASCHI

Palazzo Braschi is on a small square, Piazza San Pantaleo, off Corso Vittorio Emanuele, the main thoroughfare running from Piazza Venezia to the Vatican. The monument in the square commemorates Marco Minghetti, a well known Italian statesman of the 19th century. The palace was commissioned by Giovan Angelo Braschi who, as Pius VII, was the last pope

Palazzo Braschi.

Palazzo Farnese.

Palazzo Madama.

to have a personal residence erected in the city. Although the building actually dates from 1780, that its architect (Cosimo Morelli), was greatly influenced by 16th century palaces is clearly visible, particularly in the façade. On the other hand, the interior, especially the monumental staircase, is purely neo-Classical, the predominant style of the day. Today Palazzo Braschi houses the **Museo di Roma** (Museum of Rome) a fascinating collection of art works and relics from four centuries of Roman culture (16th through 19th). These include busts and portraits of popes, cardinals and courtiers, views of historic Rome, maiolica pottery, furniture, and even costumes.

•PALAZZO FARNESE•

Of elegant and harmonious design, Piazza Farnese is adorned with two immense granite basins removed from the Baths of Caracalla and turned into fountains by Rainaldi in 1626. The south side of the square is occupied by the Palazzo Farnese, one of the finest Renaissance buildings in Rome. It was designed by Antonio Sangallo the Younger who received the commission from Cardinal Alessandro Farnese (later Pope Paul III) in 1514, continued under the direction of Michelangelo, and completed by Giacomo della Porta. The lilies on the marvelous entablature and on the fountains are the Farnese emblem. The interior of the Palace is just as elegant as the exterior. Of special note are Sangallo's immense atrium, the arcades of the inner courtyard, and the Galleria.

On the Galleria walls are frescoes by Annibale and Agostino Carracci, the Bolognese artists, which rank among the finest painted in the 17th century. The subject of the cycle is the *Triumph of Love*. Today Palazzo Farnese is the French Embassy.

•PALAZZO MADAMA•

Palazzo Madama, the Italian Senate building since 1871, rises on the east side of Corso Rinascimento, not far from Piazza Navona. It was named after "Madame" Margaret of Austria, who was married to Alessandro de' Medici, of the famous Florentine family that built the palazzo. Work on the building started in the late 16th century and went on until the 17th century when it was completed under the direction of Ludovico Cardi and Paolo Marucelli. The Baroque façade is richly accented by gabled windows, a lively entablature, an elaborate portal with columns supporting a balcony and chimneys in bizarre shapes.

View of the Tiber Island.

•ISOLA TIBERINA•
(The Tiber Island)

The elongated shape of the *Isola Tiberina* has always been associated with an old legend which tells how the sacred snake, symbol of Esculapius, the god of healing, escaped from the boat transporting it down the Tiber, and sought refuge on the island. To commemorate the mythical event, the Romans fitted out the island as an oversize boat using an obelisk as a mast (remains are still visible), and then built a temple on it in honor of Esculapius. During the Middle Ages, the church of San Bartolomeo replaced the pagan temple.

In the 16th century, following the tradition which assigned the island to medical and healing functions, the Hospital of Saint John of God was built on the site. The single bridge span, just off the Isola Tiberina, is all that remains of a Roman bridge, the Ponte Emilio which collapsed in 1598 and was thereafter known as the Ponte Rotto (Broken Bridge).

The Broken Bridge (Ponte Rotto or Ponte Emilio).

Ponte Fabricio.

The Bridge of Sant'Angelo with Castel Sant'Angelo (Hadrian's Tomb).

•PONTE CESTIO•
(Cestio Bridge)

This bridge and the Ponte Fabricio link the Isola Tiberina to the banks of the Tiber. The Ponte Fabricio, was built in 62 B.C. shortly after the Ponte Milvio, which dates from 105 B.C. and is thus the oldest in Rome. The Ponte Cestio, first erected in 46 B.C., was named after Cestius the *Curator Viarum* (road commissioner) who had it built.

•PONTE VITTORIO EMANUELE•
(Victor Emanuel Bridge)

Situated on a wide bend in the Tiber between Ponte Sant'Angelo and Ponte Principe Amedeo di Savoia- Aosta, this imposing modern bridge dates from the turn of the century. It is adorned with statues of Winged Victories on the four great pillars at each end, and allegorical figures on the arch supports along the sides.

•PONTE SANT'ANGELO•

This bridge was built in 134 A.D. to link the Mausoleum of Hadrian (present-day Castel Sant'Angelo) to the left bank of the Tiber. The three center spans date from the original con-

Victor Emanuel Bridge.

struction, while the two on the ends were erected in the 17th century. Clement IX commissioned Gian Lorenzo Bernini to "modernize" the bridge in the middle of the 17th century. The Neapolitan master added ten statues of angels, designed new parapets, and had his pupils carry out the project. The result is one of the most spectacular architectural masterpieces of the Baroque period.

Castel Sant'Angelo (Hadrian's Tomb).

•CASTEL SANT'ANGELO•
(Hadrian's Tomb)

This immense building rises on the site of the Mausoleum of Hadrian, the so-called Hadrianeum. The huge funerary monument was built for the emperor in 130 A.D. probably by the architect Demetrianus. It is believed that Hadrian, a cultured man of varied interests, actually had a hand in the design of the building. In fact, his great love of Greek art and culture is

Castel Sant'Angelo in an engraving by the Rouargue brothers (19th century).

Main Courtyard and Cannonball Courtyard.

The Terrace of the Angel, on top of Hadrian's Tomb.

Augustus, which in turn was based on the Etruscan tumulus style tomb. The original building consisted of an immense base surmounted by a drum. Cut into the base, at the level of the bridge, was the long entrance-way or *dromos* which led to a great spiral staircase (which still exists) going up to a second corridor and the burial cells. Atop the building stood a statue of the emperor. In 271, Aurelian turned it into a stronghold encircled by protective walls. The monument was renamed in 590 when, according to legend, an angel appeared on top of it to announce that the plague epidemic would soon be over. From the medieval period on, it was the most important of the papal strongholds in Rome. Throughout the centuries it served as both a haven for the papal court in times of trouble, and an ill-famed dungeon. Among the illustrious inmates of Castel Sant'Angelo were the Renaissance artist writer Benvenuto Cellini (who somehow managed to escape), the philosopher Giordano Bruno, the alchemist Cagliostro, and in the 19th century numerous patriots of the *Risorgimento* (struggle for the unification of Italy). Today the building is a multi-story complex of interior and exterior halls and courtyards. Of special note is the main Courtyard which is also known as the Angel Court (after the statue of the angel) and the Cannonball Court (after the stone ammunitions piled up around it). The monument is majestically crowned by a gigantic 17th century bronze statue of the Angel commemorating the miraculous apparition of 590. Castel Sant'Angelo also houses a museum, the Museo Nazionale Militare e d'Arte, which includes papal apartments with their original decoration, as well as paintings and sculpture. The fine view of the city from the terrace on top of the Castel Sant'Angelo should not be missed.

reflected in several of the privately-owned buildings he commissioned, a notable example of which is his celebrated Villa of Tivoli. On the other hand, where public buildings were concerned, he stuck to simple functional designs in keeping with the prevalent architectural style of his day. In the case of the *Hadrianeum*, he chose to model it after the Mausoleum of

PIAZZA DI SPAGNA and TRINITÀ DEI MONTI

Piazza di Spagna, located at the intersection of Via del Babuino and Via Condotti, is one of the most popular spots in Rome, especially for sightseers. On the south side of the square is the imposing **Palazzo di Propaganda Fide**, begun by Bernini in the mid-17th century on a commission from Pope Urban VIII and completed by Borromini. The fountain in the middle, known as *Fontana della Barcaccia*, was designed by Bernini's father, Pietro, in 1629. The 137-step travertine staircase, (the so-called Spanish Steps) leading up to Trinità dei Monti was built by Francesco De Sanctis in 1726. Most of the time, a colorful crowd of tourists, young people, and flower sellers can be found congregating here. On the top is Piazza Trinita dei Monti, dominated by the façade of the church of the same name, in front of which rises a Roman imitation of an Egyptian obelisk known as the *Obelisco Sallustiano*. Trinità dei Monti was built in the early 16th century, although the staircase, designed by Domenica Fontana, is a later addition. Its simple façade accented by twin bell towers was designed by Carlo Maderno in the 17th century. Now property of the French government, the church contains several fine works of art, including an Assumption and Deposition by Michelangelo's pupil, Daniele da Volterra.

The Spanish Steps.

View of Piazza Navona.

The Fountain of the Moor.

The Fountain of the Rivers.

•PIAZZA NAVONA•

Picturesque Piazza Navona is a favourite haunt of Romans and non-Romans alike. Baroque in style, the oval square rises on the site of the Stadium of Domitian. Its name is a corruption of Piazza in Agone, from *agoni* (athletic contests), since from Roman times up to the middle of the 19th century it was used for horse races or flooded for mock naval battles. It contains three splendid monumental fountains: the Fontana del Moro (Moor's Fountain), was made by Giovanni Antonio Mari after designs by Bernini (mid-1600s); in the middle of the square is the *Fontana dei Fiumi* (Fountain of the Rivers), one of Bernini's masterpices. Dated 1651, it represents a cliff with personifications of rivers from four continents in dramatic poses seated around it. The rivers are the Nile, the Rio della Plata, the Ganges and the Danube. The third fountain, the *Fontana del Nettuno*, originally consisted only of the lobed pool; the sculptures which now adorn it were added at the end of the 19th century. The church of Sant'Agnese in Agone, begun by Carlo and Girolamo Rainaldi in 1652, was completed by Borromini in 1657. The unusual concave façade with its Corinthian columns is surmounted by twin bell-towers on either side of the cupola. The area encompassed by Piazza Navona, Ponte Sant'Angelo and Campo dei Fiori was for almost four centuries the center of civic life in Rome. Piazza Navona in particular where there were great open air markets and where games and festivities were held, took on the function of Forum during the Renaissance and Baroque periods.

Everyone who visits Rome notices the incredible number of fountains of all sizes and shapes scattered about the city. From Antiquity on, fountains served the dual purpose of providing water and embellishing the areas where they were located, which were generally open and public. Sometimes much bigger than ordinary fountains, they were more like pools or watering troughs. As centuries passed, changing styles and tastes altered their outward appearance, resulting in greater emphasis on their decorative as opposed to utilitarian function, yet the primary purpose of making good drinking water available to the populace was never lost sight of. They were much admired, especially during the Romantic period – the composer Ottorino Resphighi even wrote a piece in their honor. As space does not allow us to mention all of them, we shall discuss a sampling of the most important (in addition of course to the famous fountains in Piazza Navona which are described above).

The Trevi Fountain; above, *the Fontana della Barcaccia.*

•FONTANA DI TREVI•
(Trevi Fountain)

This enormous fountain occupies most of Piazza di Trevi, a charming little square off Via del Corso. It rises on the spot where the *Aqua Vergine*, the aqueduct built by Agrippa in 19 B.C. had its terminus. After centuries of abandon, the aqueduct was reactivated when, in the 1400s, Pope Nicholas V commissioned Leon Battista Alberti to design a basin in which its waters could be collected. The

decorative elements (niches, sculpture, rocks, etc.) were added in the 18th century by Niccolo Salvi, who received the commission from Pope Clement XII. An imposing figure of the god Oceanus riding a gigantic seashell drawn by seahorses dominates the elaborate naturalistic-architec-tural setting in which other figures (tritons) loll among the rocks. The Fontana di Trevi, immortalized in countless songs and films, is undoubtedly the most famous fountain in Rome, if not the world. According to tradition, throwing a coin into the water ensures a speedy return to the Eternal City.

FONTANA DELLE TARTARUGHE
(Fountain of the Turtles)

The fountain beautifully complements its lovely setting (Piazza Mattei). Despite the charming story about its having been built in a single night by a Roman aristocrat, Pietro Mattei, owner of two of the buildings on the square,

The Fountain of the Turtles; above: Detail of the Trevi Fountain.

Fountain of the Aqua Paola aqueduct.

we know that it was carved by a sculptor, Taddeo Landini, in 1584. The fountain consists of a lower level with four seated youths holding up a basin. The turtles for which the fountain was named were added by Bernini in the 17th century.

•FONTANA DELLA NAVICELLA•
(The Fountain of the Little Ship)

This unusual fountain stands in the middle of Piazza della Navicella atop the Celian Hill. The basin is actually a marble representation of an antique boat, probably a replica of a Roman sculpture. It was built in 1513, during the papacy of Leo X.

Fountain of the Navicella.

Fountain of the Triton, by Gian Lorenzo Bernini.

•FONTANA DEL TRITONE•
(Fountain of the Triton)

Situated right in the middle of one of Rome's most heavily trafficked squares, Piazza Barberini, the famous *Fontana del* *Tritone* was built in 1643 by Bernini, who was awarded the commission by Pope Urban VIII Barberini. It is acclaimed as one of finest of the many fountains designed by the great Baroque master. Here Bernini achieves a perfect blend of the stationary elements (the sculpture), and the moving ones

Synagogue.

(the jets of water). The water spurts out of a shell held by a Triton astride a larger shell which, in turn, is supported by four dolphins. The bees on the dolphins' tails are the emblem of the Barberini family.

•TEMPIO ISRAELITICO•
(The Synagogue)

The synagogue is located in the heart of one of the most characteristic quarters of Rome (the old ghetto), to which the Jews were confined between the 16th and 19th centuries. The **Porticus of Octavia** and a series of Medieval and Renaissance dwellings, some still in excellent condition, are to be found in the same area. The Synagogue of Rome, one of the most recent in Italy, was built at the beginning of this century on the basis of Assyro-Babylonian architectural models; it has a large pavilion dome covered in aluminum. The Jewish community in Rome is the largest of many in Italy. Most of the synagogues in Italy adapt the orthodox Sephardic rite. Women and men separate during religious services with the women participating from a part of the

Piazza Campo de' Fiori; below, center: The Farnesina.

temple reserved for them. The Synagogue is open to the public everyday except Saturday which is kept exclusively for religious services.

The Piazzale del Gianicolo with the monument to Garibaldi.

•PIAZZA CAMPO DE' FIORI•

This is one of the most authentically picturesque areas in the city, and the morning market in the historical piazza has a typically Roman flavor. At one time capital punishments were carried out here; among others, Giordano Bruno, philosopher and utopist, was burnt as a heretic by the Inquisition on February 17, 1600. A 19th century bronze statue in the middle of the piazza commemorates the sad event. Another characteristic Roman market which

attracts thousands of Romans and tourists alike on Sunday mornings, is that of Porta Portese. It extends over an enormous area in the streets around the ancient Porta Portese, which was rebuilt in the 17th century by Pope Urban VIII and acquired its name over the centuries. The market is very lively and colorful and you can find just about everything there: from works of art to antique books and second-hand furniture. Careful choice and skillful negotiating can earn you some real bargains.

•LA FARNESINA•

The villa was built by Baldassarre Peruzzi at the foot of the Janiculum in the early 1500s for Agostino Chigi, a wealthy banker, although it was named after the Farnese family who became its owners in 1580. Over the years it changed hands a number of times. Today it is part of a famous cultural institute, the Accademia dei Lincei, whose headquarters are in the nearby Palazzo Corsini. Inside is the celebrated *Galleria* frescoed by Raphael with mythological scenes.

•IL GIANICOLO•
(The Janiculum Hill)

One of the nicest walks in Rome is to start from the right bank of the Tiber and make the winding climb up the Janiculum Hill. Near the top there is a vast terrace overlooking the city, in the middle of which stands a *Monument to Giuseppe Garibaldi*. Proceeding, we reach the **Porta San Pancrazio,** the summit of the hill.

The Shrine to Esculapius in the park of Villa Borghese.

•VILLA BORGHESE•

The Villa Borghese is actually a huge beautifully-land-scaped park right in the heart of Rome next to the Pincio and the Gardens of Villa Medici which was originally commissioned by Cardinal Scipione Borghese in the early 1600s.. The park is full of things to see. On an islet in the middle of the artificial lake is a quaint 18th century imitation of a Greek temple dedicated to Esculapius. The Piazza di Siena Hippodrome is famous for the equestrian events that are held there. The zoo, the Borghese Gallery, the Galleria Nazionale d'Arte Moderna in the Palazzo delle Belle Arti, the Etruscan Museum of Villa Giulia in the villa of Pope Julius III, are all inside the park.

•THE PINCIO•

Overlying Piazza del Popolo is the Pincio, a public park designed by Valadier at the turn of the century. One of the most popular green spots in the city, it extends over what were once the luxuriant gardens belonging to the Roman aristocrats, among them the Pincio family after whom it was named. In addition to the busts of famous men lining the paths, there is also an unusual water clock immersed in the lush vegetation.

Temple of Faustina in the park of Villa Borghese.

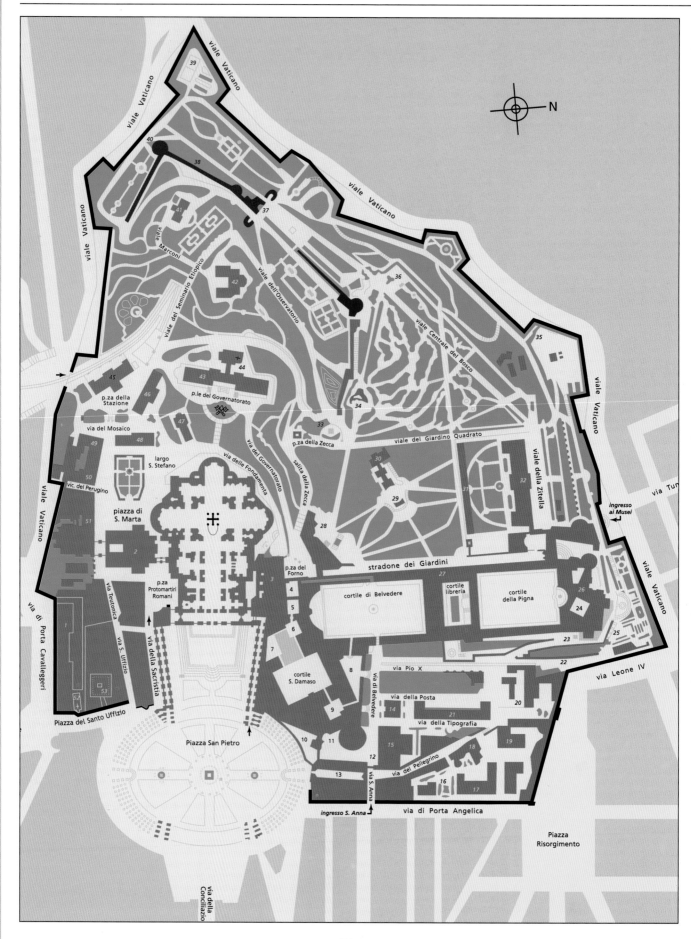

N

viale Vaticano
viale Vaticano
viale Vaticano
viale Vaticano
viale Vaticano
viale Vaticano
viale Vaticano
viale Vaticano

39
40
38
41
viale Marconi
37
viale del Seminario Etiopico
42
viale dell'Osservatorio
36
viale Centrale del Bosco
35

44
43
45
p.za della Stazione
46
p.le del Governatorato
34
33
via del Mosaico
47
p.za della Zecca
viale del Giardino Quadrato
viale della Zitella
48
49
via del Governatorato
salita della Zecca
30
32
largo S. Stefano
via delle Fondamenta
50
ingresso ai Musei
vic. del Perugino
29
31
51
28
piazza di S. Marta
viale Vaticano
2
p.za del Forno
stradone dei Giardini
27
p.za Protomartiri Romani
3
cortile di Belvedere
cortile libreria
cortile della Pigna
26
24
4
25
via della Sacristia
via Teutonica
via S. Uffizio
5
23
1
6
22
7
via di Porta Cavalleggeri
cortile S. Damaso
8
via Pio X
via di Belvedere
via Leone IV
53
52
9
via della Posta
14
20
via della Tipografia
21
10
11
15
18
19
Piazza del Santo Uffizio
12
24
via S. Anna
16
17
13
via del Pellegrino
Piazza San Pietro
ingresso S. Anna
via di Porta Angelica
Piazza Risorgimento
via della Conciliazio
via Tun

St. Peter's Square and the Basilica.

• VATICAN CITY •

To millions of people all over the world, Rome is not just a political, artistic, and historic center. To them, it is all these, but even more important, it is the capital of Catholicism, the city of the Holy Father, successor to Peter and Vicar of Christ. Catholics from every corner of the world flock to the Vatican City to pay homage to the pope and visit its holy places. In terms of territory, as everyone knows, the Vatican ranks as the tiniest state in the world. It rises on the Vatican Hill, on the right bank of the Tiber between Monte Mario and the Janiculum Hill. The origin of the name is unknown, but many scholars are convinced that it derives from a previous Etruscan settlement. In the 1st century A.D. the Emperor Caligula had a circus built on the area, then known as the "Ager Vaticanus" Nero made it into an immense park where, ironically, many early Christians were martyred. Among the martyrs, was St. Peter, in 67. He was nailed to a cross, upside down at his own request, because he felt unworthy of being crucified in the same way as Christ. Three centuries later, when Christianity had become the major religion of the Roman empire, a great church was built on the site of St. Peter's tomb, although Constantine's basilica was a far cry from the immense cathedral that would one day be the biggest and most important in Christendom. Soon numerous buildings, both civil and religious, surrounded the church dedicated to St. Peter. In the 9th century, Pope Leo IV had the whole area – referred to as the Leonine City – enclosed within protective walls so that the Holy See would not be threatened by the bloody political struggles being waged outside. Over the centuries, additional walls were built by other popes; the present ones date from the first half of the 17th century.

St. Peter's Square and the Via della Conciliazione.

St. Peter's Square; below, St. Peter's.

•PIAZZA SAN PIETRO•
(St. Peter's Square)

St. Peter's Square is reached by way of the Via della Conciliazione. The immense boulevard, built in 1937, while appropriate for handling the steady traffic flow to and from the Vatican, is cold and anonymous looking, and thus inappropriate from an aesthetic viewpoint. Unlike the roadway, however, the square is a fitting approach to the world's greatest basilica. Designed by Bernini (1656-1667), it consists of a curving double colonnade, a granite obelisk, and two fountains, designed by Carlo Maderno, placed between the colonnades and the obelisk. Each of the colonnades is composed of four rows of

Ionic columns (for a total of 284) surmounted by 96 statues of saints and martyrs. The obelisk, dating from the 1st century B.C., was brought from Egypt by Caligula who wanted to use it as a marker in his circus. In 1586 Pope Sixtus V commissioned Domenico Fontana to move it to St. Peter's. As can be imagined, this was hardly an easy task, and, in fact, the undertaking required 900 men, 150 horses, 47 cranes, and four months to complete. During the Middle Ages, it was believed that the urn inside the golden sphere atop the obelisk contained the ashes of Julius Caesar (now there is a relic of the Holy Cross).

Via della Conciliazione; below: *a group of visitors waiting for the papal audience.*

•BASILICA DI SAN PIETRO•
(St. Peter's Basilica)

Over the tomb containing the mortal remains of the Apostle Peter, the first Christians built an oratory. In 324, by order of the Emperor Constantine, a great basilica was erected on the site which was at the time occupied by the Circus of Caligula. The Constantinian basilica featured a plan with five naves and was preceded by a great atrium with a portico around it. The façade was completely covered with mosaics. Over the centuries, treasures and masterpieces continued to pour in, and the building became more and more magnificent, but, due to shifting of terrain, at a certain point it looked as though it were about to collapse. Around the middle of the 14th century, Pope Nicolas V was advised by the great architect Leon Battista Alberti to have it demolished, which he did, and Bernardo Rossellino was commissioned to design a new building in its place. Following Nicholas V's death in 1455, work on the project was suspended, and was not resumed until 1506 when Julius II named Donato Bramante chief architect. Bramante died in 1514, leaving the project unfinished. His successors were first Raphael, then Baldassarre Peruzzi, Antonio da Sangallo, and Michelangelo Buonarroti. Michelangelo changed Bramante's original plan and designed an immense dome but he died in 1564 just as construction was getting under way. The dome was completed in 1590 by Domenico

Façade of St. Peter's Basilica.

The fountain in St. Peter's Square; below: the dome of St. Peter's designed by Michelangelo.

Fontana and Carlo Della Porta. In the 18th century, Carlo Maderno was commissioned to extend the central nave and build the façade. The

façade is a majestic monumental structure which is, however somewhat monotonous with its continual alternating of columns and pillars. In the center is the window from which the Pope blesses the crowds below. On top are 13 colossal statues of *Christ, John the Baptist, and the Apostles.* The elaborate clocks on either end are by Valadier. The entrance to the Basilica is reached by way of a vast flight of stairs flanked by 19th century statues of Saints Peter and Paul. Three great portals lead to the atrium with portico completed by Maderno in 1612. Measuring 233' x 44' x 66', it is adorned with *Statues of popes* and, in the lunette of the central portal, the famous *Mosaico della Navicella* (mosaic of the little boat) made in 1298 for

Cardinal Jacopo Stefaneschi, following designs by Giotto It shows Jesus walking on the waters towards the Apostles seated in a boat. Five portals open into the church: the first one on the right is the Porta Santa (Holy Door) which is always kept closed and is ceremoniously opened every twenty-five years in celebration of the Holy Year. The door on the far left is the Porta della Morte (Door of Death), a modern work by Giacomo Manzù (1964). In the middle is the Porta del Filarete, with its superb bronze panels executed by Antonio Filarete for Pope Eugenius IV in 1433. The subjects of the bas-reliefs are, on the top row, *the Virgin and Christ enthroned,* in the center row, *St. Paul with a sword* and *St. Peter giving the keys to Pope Eugenius,* and on the lower row, *the Martyrdom of St. Paul* and *the Martyrdom of St. Peter* rendered in a lively style enriched by many classical ele-

Detail of the colonnade and dome of the Basilica; below, from left: the central door of the Basilica by Filarete and the Porta della Morte by Giacomo Manzù.

ments On the inside of the door facing the basilica the artist affixed his signature along with an odd scene showing himself astride a camel. The other doors were built using a colossal beam from the old Constantinian basilica. Saint Peter's is surmounted by an immense dome, the largest ever built. Michelangelo's design of 1547, inspired by the dome Brunelleschi had built for the cathedral of Florence a century before, was conceived as the focal point of a Greek cross (as St. Peter's had been designed according to the plan of Bramante), but when the nave was

lengthened and the Latin cross plan prevailed, the distance between the dome and the façade was increased and the dome became less prominent (and, in fact, is not visible from the square). The dome is a powerful but agile structure with prominent ribs running vertically along the outside of the cupola, set on a massive base, with great round windows set off by double columns and surmounted by an elegant lantern with cusped columns. The view from the dome (entrance from inside the church) is well worth the effort of climbing the 537 steps.

THE INTERIOR

Although the basilica has been continuously altered over the centuries and certainly cannot be considered a homogeneous creation, the first thing that strikes a person standing at the entrance is not its grandiosity, but rather the harmony of its proportions. All of the architectural, sculptural, and decorative elements have been carefully conceived to complement each other, so that the

Bronze baldaquin by Bernini and the dome by Michelangelo. Below: *The Porta Santa*.

Equestrian Statue of Charlemagne in the entrance hall of the Basilica.

result is of perfect harmony. The central nave consists of eight gigantic pillars sustaining a 143' tall barrel-vault ceiling decorated with gilded coffers and rosettes. Along the nave there are two series of statues in niches which represent the *Virtues* and various *Founders of religious orders*. The medallions supported by cherubs on the inner sides of the pillars contain portraits of the first popes and were made according to designs by Bernini. The section going from the entrance to the third row of pillars constitutes Maderno's extension, and thus the realization of the elongated Latin cross plan commissioned by Pope Paul V. The apse and crossing area, however, convey an idea of what Michelangelo's conception of space in terms of a Greek cross might have looked like. The mosaic on the pillar which supports the dome, copied from Raphael's painting of the *Transfiguration*. The High Altar, in the exact center of the crossing is enclosed by Bernini's celebrated bronze canopy structure or *Baldacchino*. The impres-

sive work, cast in bronze which had been removed from the Pantheon, was commissioned by Pope Urban VIII and begun by Bernini when he was just 26 years old. Despite its immense size, it has been designed to allow the viewer's gaze to reach all the way back to St. Peter's throne in the apse (also designed by Bernini). Below the High Altar is the *Confession*, a semi circular structure surrounded by a balustrade inside of which are 99 perpetually burning lamps illuminating the tomb of Saint Peter. Among the greatest treasures in St. Peter's are the tombs of numerous popes many of which, before their deaths, commissioned the foremost artists of their day to create sepulchral monuments worthy of such honorable burial. Two of the finest are in the apse: the tomb of Paul III Farnese, by Guglielmo della Porta, and, opposite it, the tomb of Urban VIII Barberini, created by Bernini from 1642 to 1647. The sculptural decoration of Pope Urban's tomb reveals Bernini at the height of his creative and expressive

Bronze baldaquin by Bernini.

Apse of St. Peter's Basilica.

Dome of St. Peter's designed by Michelangelo.

Main altar.

powers, a fitting tribute to the man who had fostered, protected, and patronized him throughout his long artistic career. The monument is shaped like a pyramid. The bronze figure on the top represents Pope Urban, his right hand raised in a gesture of blessing. Below, flanking the sarcophagus, are two marble figures, personifications of *Charity* and *Justice*, while *Death*, in the middle, is depicted writing the pope's name on a scroll. The Barberini bees, which Bernini had always represented neatly aligned on the family coat-of-arms, on the tomb appear, for the last time, scattered here and there. Several other papal tombs, including

Statue of St. Peter.

Left nave of the Basilica.

Right nave of the Basilica.

Chapel of the Baptismal Font.

those of John XXII, Paul VI, and John Paul I, are in the *Grotte Vaticane* (Vatican Grottoes), a vast underground chamber extending from the crossing midway down the nave, which can be reached through the passageway built into one of the pillars. Among the many

great works of art here one of the most noteworthy is the celebrated bronze statue of St. Peter which represents the Apostle seated and giving the benediction, while holding the keys, his attribute symbolizing papal authority. The right foot is visibly worn down by the kisses of the faithful, proof of the devotion expressed by centuries of pilgrims. In one of the first chapels at the entrance to the Basilica, the visitor can admire Michelangelo's Pietà. It is the only work bearing Michelangelo's signature, which is still plainly visible on the Virgin's sash. The Pietà is a masterpiece of great formal composure, perfect in the power of expression of the faces and for the accurate rendering of the details. The Virgin is depicted resigned to her boundless grief as She mourns Her Son who looks as though He is lost in a deep sleep, a prelude to His forthcoming Resurrection.

Chapel of St. Michael.

Chapel of St. Sebastian.

Interior of the Basilica.

Pietà, by Michelangelo Buonarroti.

• THE VATICAN PALACES •

By the 5th century, a building that served as a papal residence already stood next to the Constantinian Basilica of St. Peter's (although the official one was still in the Lateran). Starting in the 14th century, the palace was continuously enlarged and embellished, until it became, not one, but a complex of buildings, designed by the great architects of the 15th -17th centuries (Bramante, Bernini, Pirro Ligorio, and others). Sections of the Palazzo Apostolico Pontificio include the papal apartments, the Vatican Museums, Raphael's Stanze, and the Sistine Chapel (these will later be discussed in greater detail). One of the most noteworthy is the Cappella Niccolina built under Nicholas V, in the mid-1400s and frescoed shortly after by Fra Angelico with scenes from the lives of Saints Lawrence and Stephen. The Martyrdom of St. Stephen reveals the painter-friar's characteristic traits i.e. decorative color, minute rendering of detail, and far-reaching landscape. The Cappella Paolina, commissioned by Pope Paul III and designed by Antonio Sangallo in 1540, was frescoed by Michelangelo with scenes depicting the *Conversion of St. Paul* and the *Crucifixion of St. Peter*.

The royal stairway in the Papal Palace.

• RAPHAEL'S ROOMS •

The apartments known as the Stanze (rooms) were begun under Nicholas V in the 15th century. In 1508 Pope Julius decided it was time to complete the decoration of the rooms, and commissioned several famous artists including Signorelli and Lorenzo Lotto. When work was already in progress, the Pope heard from Bramante about a talented young painter, Raffaello Sanzio, native of Urbino. Raphael was summoned to Rome and Julius was so impressed with the youth's trial piece, he fired everyone else and awarded him the whole commission. The *Stanza dell'Incendio di Borgo* shows Pope Leo IV

Battle of Ostia, by Raphael.

The School of Athens, by Raphael.

The Room of Constantine (Stanze of Raphael).

The Liberation of St. Peter, by Raphael.

miraculously putting out a fire in the Borgo district. However the most famous frescoes are in the *Stanza della Segnatura*: these include the *Disputation of the Holy Sacrament* with its purely doctrinal content; the *School of Athens*, which is considered one of the artist's finest works, depicts the triumph of Philosophy. In the center are the figures of Plato and Aristotle, surrounded by other great philosophers; the *Parnassus*, which represents the World of the Arts, with Apollo and the Muses surrounded by Dante, Virgil and Homer and other great poets. Superb frescoes also adorn the adjacent **Stanza di Eliodoro** and the **Stanza di Constantino**.

•MUSEI VATICANI•
(Vatican Museums)

The Vatican Museums, comprising the *Pinacoteca* (painting gallery), the Museo Sacro, the Pio-Clementino Collection (Classical art), and the Egyptian and Etruscan collections, include works of art accumulated by the popes over a period of several centuries and rank as one of the finest assemblages of art works in the world. The most important sections of the Museums are those dedicated to Classical antiquity and, above all the collection of paintings or *Pinacoteca*. The Pinacoteca is

The Cortile della Pigna inside the Vatican Museums.

housed in a modern building, designed by Luca Beltrami for Pope Pius XI in the 1930s, which includes offices, storerooms, laboratories, and fifteen exhibition halls in which 460 paintings are exhibited as well as the tapestries created with designs provided by Raphael. The collection originated when the numerous works carried off by the French troops during the Napoleonic period were returned to Italy and it was decided to house them all under one roof. After Pius VIII had the Pinacoteca moved to the *Appartamento Borgia*, it was transferred to the Rooms of Pope Gregorio XIII on the third floor, the Loggia of San Damaso (1822). Subsequently the collection was moved to the Galleria degli Arazzi (Tapestry

Ariadne Sleeping.

Gallery) and then to the Rooms of Pius V, and, at long last, to its own building in 1983. Worthy of particular note is the celebrated marble group known as the *Laocoon* which was unearthed in 1506 on the site of the *Domus Aurea*, Nero's sumptuous private dwelling. Created by the Rhodian sculptor Agesander in the 2nd century B.C., it has all the dramatic intensity of the finest Hellenistic sculpture. The subject is inspired by an episode from the Trojan War. Laocoön, a Trojan, warned his fellow citizens not to allow the Greeks' wooden horse to enter the city, whereupon Apollo sent out two sea snakes to strangle him and his sons to death, and thus aid his Greek friends. The refined piece of 3rd -2nd century B.C. Hellenistic sculpture, *Sleeping Ariadne*, is suffused with a delicate sweetness. The Cretan heroine who helped Theseus escape from the Labyrinth of the Minotaur, is depicted in the gentle abandon of sleep; underneath is a sarcophagus with a *Gigan-*

Icon with Five Saints (Russian art).

Angel Musician, by Melozzo da Forlì.

Relief with Gladiators fighting wild animals (from Villa Albani). Below: *Crucifixion, by Lorenzo Monaco.*

tomachia (killing of the giants). *Madonna between Saints Dominic and Catherine of Alexandria* by Beato Angelico. Fra Angelico is a special case in the painting of his era, uniting a rigorous artistic preparation with the expression of a profound religious feeling and a candid soul which are moving even to the most skeptical viewers. He was equally capable of doing large wall paintings or miniature pieces, such as this *Madonna between Saints Dominic and Catherine of Alexandria*, painted for a manuscript. Bright colors, the fusion of tones, almost invisible brush strokes and the delicacy of the figures, shining with an internal light, make this work memorable. *Annunciation*, by Mariotto di Nardo. At first a follower of the Gothic manner of the Florentines, Orcagna, as he is called, later moved closer to the style of Lorenzo Monaco. Besides being an excellent painter, he was a talented stained glass artist. *A Franciscan taking the habit* by Giovanni di Paolo. Giovanni was a Sienese artist and did most of his work in that city, executing miniatures for sacred texts and for "la Biccherna" (a group of Sienese Magistrates which managed financial affairs). While he was aware of the new Renaissance art, he often painted landscapes rich in realistic detail which were characteristic of International Gothic. The angular and expressive people in his paintings are presented in compositional patterns already proposed by Lorenzetti and Giovanni da Milano. *The Crucifixion*, by Lorenzo Monaco. His pictorial art was based on Sienese examples, predominantly that of Agnolo Gaddi. He worked for many years as a miniaturist, illustrating manuscripts many of which are still in existence but had no difficulty moving from miniature work to much larger pieces, as the fresco in the Cappella Bartolini in S. Trinità in Florence demonstrates. His works demonstrate his ability to express "monumentality", even in the placement of figures, as is clearly shown in this *Crucifixion* which is a fragment of a *predella* (altar-step) it also demonstrates his ability in the use of delicate coloring techniques, with very fine gradation of tonality, producing exceptional effects of light. *Angel Musician*, by Melozzo da Forlì. Fate has not been kind to most of the works of Melozzo; among which the monumental painting in the apse of the church of the Santi Apostoli in Rome with the *Ascension of Christ*, begun in 1427. Unfortunately, in 1702, under Pope Clement XI, the architect Carlo Fontana was commissioned to completely renovate the church and it was decided to demolish the apse. Luckily, an attempt was made to save some fragments of the fresco, including the figure of Christ (now in the Palazzo del Quirinale), many heads of Apostles and the *Angel Musicians*. The daring foreshortening effect used in these expressive faces is well-known; the Angels, enraptured with the sound of their music are now famous and much copied. *Scenes from the Life of St. Nicholas of Bari*, by Fra Angelico. The scenes with the *Legend of St. Nicholas of Myra* are fragments of a predella. The artist shifted these events to his own times: Tuscan houses and landscapes surround a little square in the triple scene showing the birth, the conversion and the charity of the Saint. To artists of the spiritual depth of Fra Angelico everyday reality was of little importance in the face of transcendental truths and the miracles of the saints. *Coronation of the Virgin*, by the great master, Raphael, who along with Michelangelo, Caravaggio and Bernini is the artist who most contributed to mak-

ing Rome into a treasure house of priceless works of art. He trained in Urbino, his native city (between Rome and Florence), most likely under his father, Giovanni Santi, before entering Perugino's workshop in 1497. In 1504 he moved to Florence where he came into contact with the great artists then active in that city, foremost of whom was Leonardo, who had a decisive influence on his work. The most important stage in his development, however, was his long stay in Rome where his eyes were opened to two new world that of the past, Classical Antiquity, and that of the future, Michelangelo. Contended by popes, cardinals, and nobles, he never lacked commissions during his brief but splendid career. This painting of the *Coronation of the Virgin* is one of his most famous. It is divided into two separate zones, earthly and heavenly. The earthly zone contains a great flower-covered sarcophagus surrounded by the Apostles against a subtly defined background which recalls the style of Leonardo; in the heavenly zone we see Christ crowning the Madonna surrounded by bands of angels and cherubim.

Madonna and Child with Saints John the Baptist, Francis, Jerome and donor, known as the *Madonna di Foligno* by Raphael. Commissioned from the artist by Sigismondo de' Conti of Foligno, the donor who is depicted kneeling on the right, as a votive offering to the Virgin Mary for his escape from the fire which destroyed his home. In this celebrated religious master-

The Madonna of Foligno by Raphael.
Above: *Relief with a horse race at the Circus Maximus.*

piece the artist's entire formal experience is summarized in the triumphal representation of the Virgin and Child. Raphael died in Rome in 1520, at just 37 years of age. The figure of the Virgin Mary and the atmospheric effects in the landscape are particularly striking. *Stories from the life of St. Nicholas of Bari*, by Gentile da Fabriano. Representative of International Gothic, Gentile was invited to paint in Venice, Brescia, Fabriano, Siena, Orvieto and Rome. Pope Martin V employed him to execute a series of frescoes in the old Palazzo Lateranense; these were finished by Pisanello. In Gentile's work, the accuracy of design and delicacy of his painting are among the finest characteristics. For example, part of a predella or altar-step with scenes from *the Legend of St. Nicholas of Myra*: the miraculous salvation of a ship about to sink. With sails in shreds, the crew dump their cargo overboard. The stormy atmosphere is majestically rendered; perhaps it had been observed first hand by the artist on the Adriatic Sea. *St. Paul*, by Fra Bartolomeo della Porta. A Dominican friar and loyal supporter of Savonarola, using 16th century forms, he succeeds in expressing a religious intimacy evinced in the characters' calm and solemn gestures, sometimes in the brilliant colors of the Venetian school. *Martyrdom of St. Erasmus*, by Nicholas Poussin. This French artist had studied Italian art and the ancient world from his youth. An admirer of Titian and Raphael, he came to Rome in 1624 and dedicated himself to the production of enchanted landscapes, inspired by the Roman countryside, and a remarkable number of historical and sacred works, all executed with a clear and solemn equilibrium, reminiscent of classical art. *Sixtus IV and Platina* by Melozzo da Forlì. This fresco, executed in 1477, was on the wall of the Vatican Library. It was transferred on to can-

The Transfiguration by Raphael.

The Miraculous Catch tapestry based on a design by Raphael.
Below: *The Sacrifice of Lystra, tapestry based on a design by Raphael.*

vas in the first half of the 19th century. Bartolomeo Sacchi, known as Il Platina, humanist and author of "Vita dei Papi" (Lives of the Popes), was the victim of a disconcerting episode: under Pope Paul II, Sixtus IV's predecessor, he was tried, and under torture admitted the existence among the Roman humanists of a plot against the Papacy. Following this anonymous accusation, however, he obtained the position of librarian in the Vatican Library. The fresco refers to this episode. Il Platina is depicted on his knees before the Pope; the other characters are Pietro Riario, Cardinal Giuliano Della Rovere and their respective brothers, Girolamo Riario and Giovanni Della Rovere. The scene is set among noble architectural structures, creating the illusion of a perspective background. *The Transfiguration*, by Raphael. This work was commissioned in 1517 by Giuliano de' Medici, Bishop of Narbonne. Unfortunately the vast and tormented work was left unfinished by the artist's untimely death on Good Friday of April 6, 1520. In this Roman period numerous disciples (many with distinct artistic personalities of their own) collaborated with the artist on works signed by him among whom Giulio Romano, Raffaello del Colle, Giovanni da Udine, Perin del Vaga, etc. They probably completed the lower part of the painting, sketched out by Raphael (1520-22). *Holy Family*, by Francesco Mancini. A beautiful piece, with brilliant colors where the artist's attention is concentrated on underlining the calm and Olympian beauty of his characters. *The Sacrifice of Lystra*, a Flemish tapestry based on a design by Raphael. It is part of a series of ten tapestries ordered by Leo X to cover the paintings in the Sistine Chapel on grand occasions. *Deposition*, by Caravaggio, painted between 1602 and 1604. It is among the artist's best works; for the pitiless objectiveness of the representation, the power and effectiveness of the compositional rhythm, and the dramatic force of the scene itself it was one of the most influential paintings of the 17th century.

•LOGGE DI RAFFAELLO•
(Vatican Loggia by Raphael)

From 1513 to 1518 Raphael worked on the architectural layout and pictorial decoration of the Vatican Loggias, planned and begun by Bramante in 1512. These constitute the second story of the façade of the Palazzo of Nicholas III looking over the Courtyard of St. Damasus and forming a series of thirteen arcades. In this project, the desire to create a synthesis between lighting and decoration is the basis of Raphael's esthetic planning, and the eighth arcade, depicting *Moses Saved from the Waters*, clearly betrays the hand of the master. In the abundant and exquisite ornamentation of the Loggias Raphael sought to imitate Roman wall decoration, in the style which much later was to be called "Pompeian".

The Loggia of Raphael.

Detail of the stucco decorations of the Loggia by Raphael.

Finding of the Infant Moses (School of Raphael).

• THE SISTINE CHAPEL •

*T*he Sistine Chapel was built by order of Sixtus IV between 1473 and 1480 by Giovannino de' Dolci, perhaps following plans by Pontelli. It consists of a rectangular hall 131 feet long, 42 feet wide and 66 feet high, illuminated by twelve windows with large lunettes sustaining the curve of the barrel-vaulted ceiling. The pavement is a splendid example of Cosmatesque art, and the elegant marble transenna or lattice-work screen, which divides off one-quarter of the chapel, is the work of Mino da Fiesole. This division serves during papal functions to separate the college of the cardinals from the papal court dignitaries. The choir, also decorated by Mino da Fiesole, has had among its choristers the great musician Pier Luigi da Palestrina. In the chapel the most important functions take place in the presence of the Pope, dignitaries of the papal court and diplomatic corps and members of the Roman aristocracy; this is also where they hold the conclave, which is the meeting of the cardinals after the death of a pope to elect his successor. When a cardinal reaches a majority of two-thirds plus one of the votes, he is elected pope: it is then that the white smoke from the stove placed in the chapel for the occasion, with its flue issuing from the last window at the end, announces the election of the new pontiff. When, on the other hand, the necessary majority has not been reached, a puff of black smoke announces that the election has not yet taken place. The Sistine is thus unique in the world from a historical point of view as well as a religious one, considering that popes have been elected here for over five-hundred years and that enormous contributions have been made by the popes to religion, civilization and art. The frescoes of the Sistine Chapel have been returned to their former splendor after undergoing extensive restorations which lasted from 1981 until the 1990s.

The Punishment of the Sons of Korah by Sandro Botticelli.

The side walls of the Chapel are covered with frescoes by great Umbrian and Florentine artists who paved the way for the three greatest geniuses of art, Michelangelo, Raphael and Leonardo da Vinci.

Depicted in twelve great panels are, on one side, *Scenes from the life of Jesus,* and on the other, *Scenes from the life of Moses,* representing the New and the Old Testaments. Beginning from the altar, the scenes from the life of Moses represent first *Moses' Trip into Egypt,* painted by Perugino (1445-1523) and Pinturicchio (1454-1513); then *The Youth of Moses,* by Sandro Botticelli (1445-1510), remarkable for the gracefulness of the two female figures (the daughters of Jethro), in which the artist achieves the beauty and lightness of touch of the Three Graces of his famous painting, *Primavera.* This is followed by *The Crossing of the Red Sea,* by Cosimo Rosselli (1439-1507), *Moses receives the Tables of the Law on Mount Sinai* and the *Adoration of the Golden Calf,* by Cosimo Rosselli, and The *Punishment of the Sons of Korah,* by Sandro Botticelli. In this last work can be seen some of the monuments of Imperial Rome: the Arch of Constantine and the Septizonium of Septimius Severus. Closing the series is the panel depicting *The Testament and Death of Moses before the Promised Land,* by Signorelli (1441-1523); this is an admirable fresco which anticipates, though in a minor key, the plastic strength of Michelangelo's figures. On the opposite side, beginning from the altar, the first *Scenes from the life of Christ* are the *Baptism of Christ,* by Perugino, perhaps

Testament and Death of Moses entering the promised Land, by Luca Signorelli.

with the collaboration of Pinturicchio, and *The Healing of the Leper and the Temptations of Christ*, by Sandro Botticelli. In the latter fresco, the artist has again depicted a Roman monument, the Hospital of S. Spirito, erected by Pope Sixtus IV. This is followed by *The Calling of Peter and Andrew*, by Ghirlandaio (1449-1494); *The Sermon on the Mount*, by Cosimo Rosselli, with the collaboration of Piero di Cosimo (1462-1521); and *The Donation of the Keys to St. Peter*, by Piero Vannucci, called Perugino, with the help of Luca Signorelli. This fresco is without doubt the most monumental of Perugino's works and certainly inspired the young Raphael in his famous painting of the *Nuptials of the Virgin* (Brera Gallery, Milan). Closing the series is *The Last Supper*, by Cosimo Rosselli.

THE CEILING (1508-1512)

In 1508 Julius II commissioned Michelangelo to decorate the vault of the ceiling. The artist's attitude toward this task is well know especially through the account given by Vasari. At the time Michelangelo was trying to organize his complex ideas for the funeral monument for Julius II, which, as it turned out, was the most dramatic problem in the artist's life. His intention was to create a work in which architecture and sculpture were combined to create a new concept of space which would renew the old system of proportions. The reluctance of Michelangelo, who signed himself "Michelangelo sculptor", to abandon such a project in order to dedicate

himself to a work of painting is therefore understandable. Initially, in both Michelangelo's project and the Pope's idea for the chapel, an architectural system was planned, with rectangular and lozenge-shaped compartments supported on the sides by the twelve figures of the apostles, placed like a series of caryatids: a study of this original project is conserved in the British Museum. In May 1508, Michelangelo went to Florence in search of capable assistants, one of whom was a close friend, Bugiardini. Thus the project began, but Michelangelo soon judged the work "a miserable thing", obtained the Pope's permission to paint the lunettes and spandrels, and sent his modest Florentine helpers home. He then abandoned the simple original plan and developed a complex symbolic series of illustrations linked to the paintings on the walls below which represent the *Lives of Jesus and Moses*. The scenes painted on the ceiling of the Sistine are meant to represent symbolically the course of human events from the Creation through the Book of Genesis towards the revelation of God the Father and Creator. Thus, below the events of Genesis, depicted in the compartments on the ceiling, are placed the *Prophets*, *Sibyls* and *Ancestors* of Christ, who announced His coming. The relationship between the Prophets and Sibyls and the panels which depict the phases of the Creation of the world represent one of the supreme moments in the history of art. Michelangelo was able to create an autonomous system of figures which was analogous to that which he had envisioned for the tomb of Julius II. One might say that the figures that he was unable to sculpture in

Overall view of the Sistine Chapel.

The Flood (vault of the Sistine Chapel).

The Original Sin (vault of the Sistine Chapel).

The Creation of Adam (vault of the Sistine Chapel).

The Sybil of Cumae.

The Sistine Chapel.

marble for the tomb he was able to sculpture with his paintbrush on the ceiling of the Chapel. The extreme simplicity of the ceiling structure not only did not turn out to be a limitation, but actually became the indispensable tool for the creation of a new spatial concept and its use as a decorative element. In fact, the lunettes become fundamental in binding the architectural elements, for turning over the view of the figures from the vertical position (*the Sibyls, Prophets, Ancestors*), to the horizontal position (*Scenes from the Creation*) by means of the nudes which act as the pivots for the rotation of the other figures. Michelangelo began by painting the entrance wall with the *Stories of Noah*, in which some uncertainties in perspective can be noted, because the artist had not realized the effect it created seen from a distance. In the second part he achieved greater pictorial synthesis, terminating in the gigantic figure of Jonah. This immense fresco (measuring some 5500 square feet) constitutes the most important document in tracing the maturing of the great artist's style, a style dominated by the classical equilibrium between form and content and still linked, in the anatomical structures and representation of landscapes and objects, to the real world. His human figures are executed in plastic terms, almost "in the round", and placed in their specially created architectural space, which makes them stand out and exalts them. Proceeding from the altar towards the door, the opposite direction from that in which they were painted, there are nine scenes: *God separating the Light from the Darkness, God creating the Sun, Moon and Planets, God separating the Earth from the Waters, the Creation of Adam; the Creation of Eve, the Original Sin and the Expulsion from the Earthly Paradise, the Sacrifice of Noah, the Flood*, and *the Drunkenness of Noah*. The execution of the fresco can be divided into separate periods: from 1508 to 1509 the stories of Noah and the corresponding

Prophets, Sibyls and Ancestors were done; in 1511 the remaining scenes were painted, and in 1512 the lunettes. The work was completed on October 31, 1512. They were four long years spent in extreme discomfort on top of scaffolding, during which Michelangelo suffered all sorts of indignities and mistreatment and yet created another of his miracles of art.

THE LAST JUDGMENT (1536-1541)

Pope Paul III Farnese, in imitation of his Medici predecessor, Clement VII, ordered Michelangelo to begin work on the painting of the *Last Judgment*, the design for which he had seen in the artist's studio at Macel de' Corvi. In June or July 1536, Michelangelo began preparing the wall on which he was to paint: two windows had to be walled over and the existing paintings scraped off. Then the wall was shaped so as to create a slant of about 24 inches from top to bottom in order to avoid dust settling on it. This created a surface 43 feet wide and 56 feet high, a total of more than 2400 square feet, on which Michelangelo painted his gigantic figures: Jesus Christ is 8' 3" high, St. Peter 8' 4" and St. Bartholomew 8' 6". The planning and execution of the great fresco took about six years: in fact the work was unveiled on November 1, 1541. The profoundly dramatic meaning of this grandiose work lies in the eschatological message of the Second Coming of Christ and the passage from the judgment of humanity as a whole to an individual, personal judgment. The figure of Christ is the pivot from which the swirling movement of the entire universe is generated, a movement which attracts the figures of the Blessed and repels those of the Damned. Another fulcrum from which the action of the immense composition derives movement is the group of

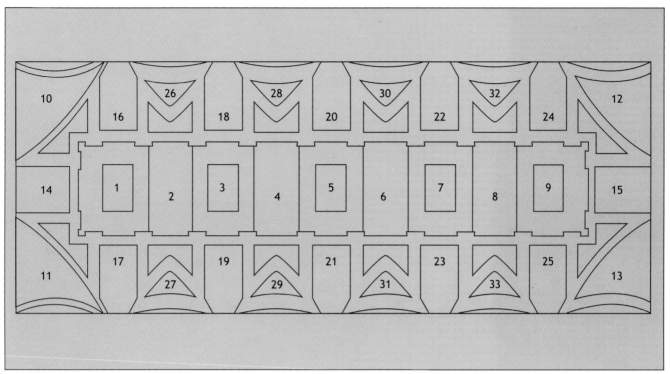

List of subjects represented in the vault of the Sistine Chapel.

1 The separation of light from darkness
2 The creation of the sun and moon
3 The separation of the waters
4 The creation of man
5 The creation of woman
6 The original sin and expulsion from Paradise
7 The sacrifice of Noah
8 The flood
9 The drunkeness of Noah
10 The hanging of Aman ordered by Esther
11 The Hebrews attacked by the serpents sent by God
12 David in the act of beheading Goliath
13 Judith with the head of Holofernes
14 The prophet Jonah
15 The prophet Zachary
16 The prophet Jeremiah

17 The Libyan Sybil
18 The Persian Sybil
19 The Prophet Daniel
20 The Prophet Ezekiel
21 The Cumaean Sybil
22 The Eritrean Sybil
23 The Prophet Isaiah
24 The Prophet Joel
25 The Delphic Sybil
26 The child Solomon with his mother
27 The future King Jesse with his parents
28 The child Rehoboam with his mother
29 The child Asa with his parents
30 The child Uzziah with his parents and a brother
31 The child Hezekiah with his parents
32 The child Zerubbabel with his parents
33 The child Josiah with his parents

Angels below the figure of Christ in Judgment who, having received the order, are sounding the trumpets to call all men to the Last Judgment. Thus the terrible fury of the Dies Irae begins. The colors are reduced almost to a monochrome seen against a strong light; the violently twisting bodies, with details foreshortened and unexpectedly overturned, and the exasperated deformation of the anatomical structures express a hitherto unseen vision of pain and terror; the contrast between the agitated movement of some figures and the dismayed stillness of others clearly renders the tragedy of all humanity. Michelangelo wrote, concerning this fresco:

"With great humility and great tedium,
with false concepts and great danger to the soul,
so came I to sculpture here things divine".

And in fact the work was greeted with "wonder and astonishment", as Vasari recounts though criticism was not lacking, above all for the nudes. Besides Biagio da Cesena whom Michelangelo depicted in the figure of Minos, another detractor from the work was the licentious and loquacious Pietro Aretino. Unfortunately the criticism of Michelangelo's frescoes in the Sistine was so violent that Pope Hadrian VI even con-

ERITHRAEA

The Eritrean Sybil.

sidered scraping the ceiling and Paul IV knocking down the wall, while Clement VIII, who wanted to whitewash the frescoes was dissuaded only by a timely protest from the Academy of S. Luca. This reaction was finally reduced to the intervention of Daniele da Volterra, limited to painting breeches on some of the nudes, which earned him the nickname of "il Braghettone" (the Trouser Man). But the passage of time, humidity, smoke from the candles, and various re-paintings altered and damaged the splendor of the original painting. After a long and complicated restoration the *Last Judgement*, rightly considered another of Michelangelo's "miracles of art" has now been restored to its original brilliance.

The Last Judgement.

Christ in judgement with the Virgin, detail of the Last Judgement.

Tivoli is situated on a hillside by the banks of the Aniene River. Among the many eminent Romans who sojourned in the splendid villas built as patrician country homes were Julius Caesar, Augustus. and Trajan and Hadrian. Hadrian's Villa, located in the environs, was the most celebrated in ancient Rome. Roman Tivoli was also renowned as the site of numerous temples, although little remains even of the largest which was consecrated to Hercules. The town and its surroundings regained great popularity during the Renaissance period when many new estates were commissioned by wealthy princes and prelates. Severely damaged in World War II, present-day Tivoli has a mostly modern appearance. The main sights are the Villa d'Este, the Cathedral, which dates from the Romanesque period and which has some notable 12th - 13th century works, the Roman temples, and the Villa Gregoriana Park.

Above: *the Fountain of the Organ* (Villa d'Este).
The Fountain of Tivoli, also called the Fontana dell'Ovato (Villa d'Este).

Road of the Hundred Fountains (Villa d'Este).

•VILLA D'ESTE•

The 16th century villa has a magnificent Italian style garden which is one of the most famous in the world. It was originally a Benedectine monastery which Cardinal Ippolito I d'Este commissioned Pirro Ligorio to remodel as his personal residence. The project which included landscaping the grounds, took the Neapolitan architect almost twenty years to complete (1550-69). The park is considered one of the finest examples of the so-called giardino all'Italiana with its geometric design. Its outstanding features are its fountains, of which there are over five hundred; on Summer evenings they are almost all illuminated and the effect is spectacular. The most striking fountains are: Fontana dell'Ovato, symbolizing the city of Tivoli; the Fontana dell'Organo, named for the water-powered organ it was once equipped with; the Fontana del Bicchierone, attributed to Bernini: the Fontana dei Draghi, with its incredibly powerful jet of water; and the Fontana della Rometta in which the Tiber Island and other Roman symbols were re-created. Among the most remarkable sights are the spouts of the "one hundred fountains" lining the viale delle Cento Fontane.

• HADRIAN'S VILLA •

This enormous and magnificent villa commissioned by Hadrian, among the most cultured of the Roman emperors, was built between 118 and 134 A.D. Countless masterpieces of ancient art were used to adorn the buildings and grounds where also reconstructions of famous places the emperor had visited on his travels to Athens, Egypt and Thessaly. Many works are on display in Roman museums. Among the main sights are the so-called *Pecile*, (so-named as it had erroneously been thought identical to a portico in Athens) an immense quadriporticus (762' x 318') around a pool and the Nymphaeum on the island, an elegant round building encircled by a portico of Ionic columns and a kind of moat; inside of this there are the ruins of a small villa which once stood on the island and is believed to have been Hadrian's personal residence. A large size nymphaeum and a building with an original shape including three exedra make up another architectural complex. There were two baths: the small baths had an elliptical hall, a circular room, and an octagonal domed structure looking oddly Baroque whereas the larger ones consisted of a vast cross-vaulted room (perhaps the *Frigidarium* or cold water baths). The most interesting remains of the maze-like Imperial Palace belong to the huge peristyle known as Piazza d'Oro (Golden plaza) and an elegant hall known as the Sala dei Pilastri Dorici (Room of the Doric pillars). The Canopus, a 390' x 58' pool in the middle of a natural valley, was named after the place near Alexandria in Egypt that inspired it. On one side of the pool is a semicircular row of columns, opposite which stands the great niche of a nymphaeum. The four caryatids nearby that probably once sustained an arbor, are copies of those belonging to the Erechtheion in Athens. Not far from the Canopus is a museum in which, among the sculpture displayed, is a fine copy of the Amazon of Phidias.

On top: *the Canopus of Villa Adriana.*
Above: *the Little Baths.*

Roughly speaking, Ostia in Antiquity was the territory which covered the area around the mouth of the Tiber, from Rome to the Tyrrhenian coast between Fregene and Laurento; i.e. the extreme north-west of ancient Latium, bordered on the north by southern Etruria. In order to be able to understand this area it is important that the visitor bear in mind, even if just visiting the excavations in Ancient Ostia, that its appearance in Antiquity was totally different from what we see today. This is not limited to the superficial appearance of the terrain which is now covered with vegetation, numerous small towns and scattered houses, where once there were marshes, salt-pans and sandy areas, but includes the geographic configuration, which has been changed over 15 centuries by variations in the course of the Tiber and the advance of the coastline due to the accumulation of silt carried downstream by the river to the sea. In Antiquity, when the river had almost got to the sea it inverted its course to form a long narrow loop with a brief straight section at the end which connected with the Tyrrhenian Sea. A flood some centuries ago caused the Tiber to change its course and from the beginning of the ancient loop it now flows straight into the Sea. For this reason the Ostia area today only faces the Tiber in part, while in Antiquity its immense warehouses lined the banks of the river which have since been worn away by erosion and floods. Because of these changes the city of Ostia, which was on the coast, is now 1.8 miles from the sea, and the port of Claudius and Trajan, once the largest in Latium, is now high and dry and many of its impressive structures are buried and sealed forever under the installations of Fiumicino Airport. Ostia originated as a 4th century B.C. Roman settlement and soon became a wealthy trading center. The recent excavations that have unearthed virtually all of the Roman town reveal its typical grid plan, along which ran the main road, the Decumanus Maximus. The center of city life was, of course, the forum, with its great temples, the 2nd century A.D.

Mask sculptures from the theatre.

Capitolium, the Temple of Roma and Augustus, the Curia, and the huge baths. Another focal point was the Piazzale delle Corporazioni, the plaza where the seventy artisan, trade, and navigation guilds had their offices. In the middle of the square is the foundation of the Temple of Ceres. with the theater nearby. The other excavated buildings comprise temples (including a round 3rd century A.D. structure), shops, dwellings, villas, baths (those named after Neptune have fine mosaics). and a late 1st century A.D. Synagogue. Sculpture and mosaics are displayed in the Museo Ostiense (Museum of Ostia). In the town of Ostia Antica (founded in 827) is an imposing Castle built by Baccio Pontelli in 1486.

Details of mosaic decorations.

INDEX